DARK PSYCHOLOGY

UNDERSTANDING MANIPULATION, PERSUASION, DECEPTION AND COVERT NLP TECHNIQUES

SUSHMITA DUTTA

TRUE SIGN
PUBLISHING HOUSE

Published by True Sign Publishing House
Address: SY. No. 21/2 & 21/3, Sonnenahalli,
Krishnarajapura, Bengaluru,
Karnataka - 560049 India
E-mail: truesignbooks@gmail.com
Website: www.truesign.in

Dark Psychology: Understanding Manipulation, Persuasion, Deception And Covert Nlp Techniques

Author: Sushmita Dutta

ISBN: 978-93-5904-208-4

First Edition: 2023

CONTENTS

INTRODUCTION **5**

1. WHAT IS PSYCHOLOGY? 7
2. WHAT IS DARK PSYCHOLOGY? 14
3. THE DARK PSYCHOLOGY TRIAD 19
4. EFFECTS AND IMPACT OF DARK PSYCHOLOGY 29
5. DARK PSYCHOLOGY: MANIPULATION AND MIND CONTROL 32
6. DECEPTION 41
7. HYPNOSIS 50
8. PROBLEM BEHAVIORS 56
9. REVERSE PSYCHOLOGY 65
10. LOVE AND RELATIONSHIPS 72
11. THE DARK FACTOR OF PERSONALITY 83
12. HOW TO PROTECT YOURSELF FROM EMOTIONAL MANIPULATION? 86
13. WHAT IS PERSUASION? 95
14. MODES OF PERSUASION 101
15. WHAT IS NEURO-LINGUISTIC PROGRAMMING (NLP)? 108

16. NEURO-LINGUISTIC PROGRAMMING (NLP) CONTD... 113

17. EXPLOITATION OF PSYCHOLOGICAL VULNERABILITIES 119

18. DIFFERENCE BETWEEN PERSUASION AND MANIPULATION 125

19. WHAT IS MEDIA MANIPULATION? 131

20. THE ROLE OF DEFENSE 138

21. BRAINWASHING 140

CONCLUSION 146

INTRODUCTION

Dark psychology is the study of human behavior from a scientific perspective. It involves using research methods such as observational studies, psychological tests, surveys and interviews to gain insight into how people act and think. It looks at both conscious and unconscious processes in order to better understand why people do the things they do.

Most people know that psychology is the systematic study of the human mind and behavior. However, few people are aware of dark psychology, which is a branch of psychological study that deals with the more nefarious aspects of human behavior. It can encompass everything from manipulation and deception to outright aggression and violence, often in the pursuit of personal gain.

Dark psychology focuses on understanding, analyzing, and manipulating people's behavior. It has been around for centuries, but it is becoming increasingly popular as the world grows more complex and interconnected. It's a topic that is shrouded in mystery and misunderstanding, covering the darker aspects of human nature, such as, manipulation, mind control and persuasion.

In this book, we will explore all facets of dark psychology and rather than telling you what to do, it will give you the ability to form effective manipulation strategies, whatever your goals and situation. After reading this book, you can expect to have greater insight into your own actions and the actions of others. You will have a strong grounding in the mechanics of manipulation, allowing you to make your own decisions about manipulating others, and recognize when others are manipulating you. While psychology is the study of human behavior and is central to our thoughts, actions, and interactions, dark psychology is the phenomenon by which people use tactics of motivation, persuasion, manipulation, and coercion to get what they want. Dark psychology is the use of psychological principles of persuasion, frame control, and emotional control in ways that harms others.

Dark psychology examines the motivations and behaviors of people who use manipulation and mind control. It is rooted in the four dark personality traits: narcissism, Machiavellianism, psychopathy, and sadism. Psychological manipulation techniques include gaslighting, projection, isolation, positive and negative reinforcement, punishment, nagging and mind control. Manipulators use lies, denial, minimization, diversion, and guilt tripping to control their victims.

This book looks at these traits, manipulation techniques, and behavioral tendencies of manipulators, and provides methods to defend against manipulation and exploitation.

CHAPTER 1

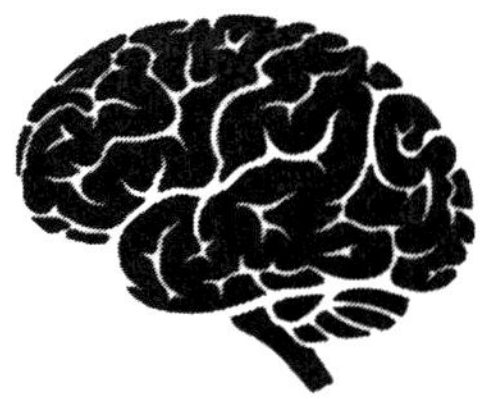

WHAT IS PSYCHOLOGY?

According to the **American Psychological Association,** psychology is the study of the mind, how it works, and how it affects behavior.

Psychology is a multifaceted discipline and includes many areas of study such as human development, sports, health, clinical, social behavior and cognitive processes. Gaining a richer and deeper understanding of psychology can help people achieve insights into their own actions as well as a better understanding of other people.

History of Psychology

Psychology is a new science, with most advances happening over the past 150 years or so. However, its origins can be traced back to ancient Greece, 400 – 500 years BCE.

The word **"psychology"** is derived from the Greek word "psyche", literally meaning **"life"** or **"breath."**

In 387 BCE, Plato suggested that the brain is where mental processes take place, and in 335 BCE **Aristotle** suggested that it was the heart.

Avicenna, a Muslim doctor, born in 980 AD, studied and treated epilepsy, nightmares, and poor memory. The first hospitals treating psychiatric conditions were said to have been set up by Islamic doctors in medieval times.

In 1774, **Franz Mesmer** proposed that hypnosis, or "mesmerism," might help cure some types of mental illness.

In 1793, **Philippe Pinel** released the first patients with mental health problems from confinement in a move that signalled a move towards more humane treatment.

In 1879, **Wilhelm Wundt**, Germany, founded psychology as an independent experimental field of study. He set up the first laboratory that carried out psychological research exclusively at Leipzig University. He is known today as the father of psychology.

In 1890, an American philosopher, **William James,** published a book entitled **'Principles of Psychology'.** It was discussed by psychologists worldwide for many decades. In the same year, New York state passed the **State Care Act**, in which people with mental health problems were to leave poor houses and enter the hospital for treatment.

Sigmund Freud, who lived from 1856 to 1939, introduced the field of psychoanalysis, a type of psychotherapy. He used interpretive methods, introspection, and clinical observations to gain understanding of the mind. He focused on resolving unconscious conflict, mental distress, and psychopathology. Freud argued that the unconscious was responsible for most of people's thoughts and behavior, and for mental health problems.

E. B Titchener, an American, strongly believed in structuralism, which focuses on the question: "What is consciousness?" **William James** and **John Dewey** were strong believers in functionalism, which addressed "What is consciousness for?"

The debate between the functionalists and structuralists led to a rapid growth in interest in psychology in the United States and elsewhere, and the establishment of the first psychology laboratory in the U.S., at Johns Hopkins University.

Major Schools of Thought in Psychology

Structuralism: Wundt and Titchener's structuralism was the earliest school of thought, but others soon began to emerge.

Functionalism: The early psychologist and philosopher William James became associated with a school of thought known as functionalism, which focused its attention on the purpose of human consciousness and behavior.

Psychoanalysis: Soon, these initial schools of thought gave way to several dominant and influential approaches to psychology. Sigmund Freud's psychoanalysis centered on how the unconscious mind impacted human behavior.

Behaviorism: The behavioral school of thought turned away from looking at internal influences on behavior and sought to make psychology the study of observable behaviors.

Humanistic psychology: Later, the humanistic approach centered on the importance of personal growth and self-actualization.

Cognitive psychology: By the 1960s and 1970s, the cognitive revolution spurred the investigation of internal mental processes such as thinking, decision-making, language development, and memory.

While these schools of thought were sometimes perceived as competing forces, each perspective has contributed to our understanding of psychology.

Branches of Psychology

Psychology is a broad and diverse field that encompasses the study of human thought, behavior, development, personality, emotion, motivation, and more. Some of the major areas of research and application within psychology are:

Clinical psychology

Clinical psychology integrates science, theory, and practice in order to understand, predict and relieve problems with adjustment, disability, and discomfort. It promotes adaption, adjustment, and personal development.

A clinical psychologist concentrates on the intellectual, emotional, biological, psychological, social, and behavioral aspects of human performance throughout a person's life, across varying cultures and socio-economic levels.

Clinical psychology can help us to understand, prevent, and alleviate psychologically-caused distress or dysfunction, and promote an individual's well-being and personal development.

Psychological assessment and psychotherapy are central to the practice of clinical psychology, but clinical psychologists are often also involved in research, training, forensic testimony, and other areas.

Cognitive psychology

Cognitive psychology investigates internal mental processes, such as problem solving, memory, learning, and language. It looks at how people think, perceive, communicate, remember, and learn. It is closely related to neuroscience, philosophy, and linguistics.

Cognitive psychologists look at how people acquire, process, and store information. Practical applications include how to improve memory, increase the accuracy of decision-making, or how to set up educational programs to boost learning.

Developmental psychology

This is the scientific study of systematic psychological changes that a person experiences throughout life, often referred to as human development.

It focuses not only on infants and young children but also teenagers, adults, and older people. Factors include motor skills, problem solving, moral understanding, acquiring language, emotions, personality, self-concept, and identity formation.

It also looks at innate mental structures against learning through experience, or how a person's characteristics interact with environmental factors and how this impacts development. Developmental psychology overlaps with fields such as linguistics.

Evolutionary psychology

Evolutionary psychology looks at how human behavior, for example, language has been affected by psychological adjustments during evolution.

An evolutionary psychologist believes that many human psychological traits are adaptive in that they have enabled us to survive over thousands of years.

Forensic psychology

Forensic psychology involves applying psychology to criminal investigation and the law.

A forensic psychologist practices psychology as a science within the criminal justice system and civil courts. It involves assessing the psychological factors that might influence a case or behavior and presenting the findings in court.

Health psychology

Health psychology is also called medical psychology. It observes how behavior, biology, and social context influence illness and health.

A physician often looks first at the biological causes of a disease, but a health psychologist will focus on the whole person and what influences their health status. This may include their socio-economic status, education, and background, and behaviors that may have an impact on the disease, such as compliance with instructions and medication.

Health psychologists usually work alongside other medical professionals in clinical settings.

Neuropsychology

Neuropsychology looks at the structure and function of the brain in relation to behaviors and psychological processes. A neuropsychology may be involved if a condition involves lesions in the brain, and assessments that involve recording electrical activity in the brain.

A neuropsychological evaluation is used to determine whether a person is likely to experience behavioral problems following suspected or diagnosed brain injury, such as a stroke.

The results can enable a doctor to provide treatment that may help the individual achieve possible improvements in cognitive damage that has occurred.

Occupational psychology

Occupational or organizational psychologists are involved in assessing and making recommendations about the performance of people at work and in training.

They help companies to find more effective ways to function, and to understand how people and groups behave at work. This can help improve effectiveness, efficiency, job satisfaction, and employee retention.

Social psychology

Social psychology uses scientific methods to understand how social influences impact human behavior. It seeks to explain how feelings, behavior, and thoughts are influenced by the actual, imagined or implied presence of other people.

A social psychologist looks at group behavior, social perception, non-verbal behavior, conformity, aggression, prejudice, and leadership. Social perception and social interaction are seen as key to understanding social behavior.

CHAPTER 2

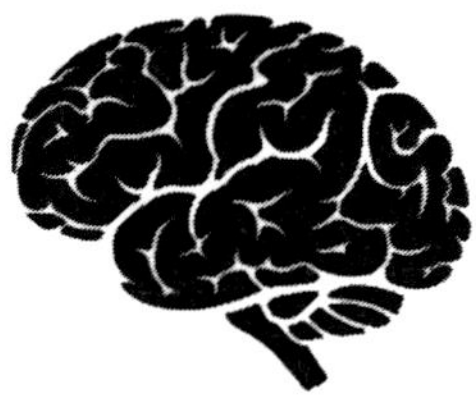

WHAT IS DARK PSYCHOLOGY?

Dark psychology refers to the dark side of human nature, such as manipulation, deception, and guilt-tripping. It is a branch of psychology that is primarily used to manipulate others. It explores the darker aspects of the human psyche, including topics such as aggression, cruelty, sadism, and psychopathy.

Generally, psychology focuses on human thoughts, behaviors, emotions and actions. However, dark psychology focuses on strategies, tactics and techniques of manipulation, persuasion, coercion and motivation that can help a person to gain what they wish for. Using these strategies can empower someone to control another person without making the victim aware of their intentions or actions. It is not only beneficial for the person who uses these strategies, whether ethically or unethically, it can also restrict the abilities and independence of the victim and may even be harmful for them. It looks at both conscious and unconscious processes in order to better understand why people do the things they do.

Core Concepts of Dark Psychology

Dark psychology is based on two key principles: manipulation and persuasion. Manipulation involves using one's power or influence to gain control over another person; it often relies on deception or coercion. Persuasion involves attempting to convince someone to believe in a certain idea or change their opinion through logical arguments or emotional appeals. Both are forms of influence that are used in dark psychology.

Another key concept in dark psychology is the use of psychological tactics to influence behavior or decision-making. These tactics can range from subtle hints or suggestions to more overt forms of manipulation such as fearmongering. The goal is always to get someone else to do what you want them to do, even if it goes against their own best interests.

Applications of Dark Psychology

Dark psychology has many applications in both personal and professional settings. On a personal level, it can be used for purposes such as self-advancement or manipulation of others for one's own gain. Professionally, it can be used for marketing purposes (e.g., creating persuasive ads), sales techniques (e.g., giving discounts), and negotiations (e.g., getting a better deal). It can also be used by law enforcement officers during interrogations or by politicians during debates and speeches—in both cases with the aim of persuading an audience in one direction or another.

Analyzing People with Dark Psychology

Using dark psychology can help us understand why people do the things they do. For example, it may help us understand why someone behaves a certain way or why they make certain decisions. Dark psychology can also be used to predict future behaviors based on past behaviors. This can be useful in many situations such as predicting customer behavior or predicting employee performance.

Dark psychology also helps us identify patterns in people's behavior that may not be obvious at first glance. By looking at these patterns over time, we can better understand why people make certain decisions or behave in certain ways. Additionally, dark psychology allows us to look at how different factors such as upbringing or culture can affect someone's decision-making process or their overall behavior.

Finally, dark psychology is an invaluable tool for understanding and analyzing human behavior from a scientific perspective. It allows researchers to gain deeper insight into why people act the way they do by studying both conscious and unconscious processes over time. By utilizing dark psychology techniques, researchers are able to better predict future behaviors based on past behaviors as well as identify patterns in people's behavior that may not be immediately obvious.

Examples of Dark Psychology

While dark psychology can be used for malicious purposes, it mustn't be confused with persuasion, which can be employed for more mundane goals, such as sales or marketing.

Examples of dark psychology can be seen across all aspects of life. While it's arguably more common in love relationships, one can also notice its use elsewhere. This could include:

- A friend uses suggestive techniques to persuade you to do something
- A power play at work, where a colleague engages in one-upmanship

Given below are additional examples of it in action:

1. Persuasive speech

Manipulative speakers often use dark psychology techniques to convince their audience to do something, whether it's buying a product, voting for a candidate, or supporting a cause. Such ("dark") persuasion often relies on emotional appeal and logical fallacies to make its case, rather than sound reasoning.

2. Deceptive advertising

Ads that rely on false claims or misleading images employ dark psychology to encourage people to take action, which may or may not be in their best interests.

3. Coercive interrogation

This technique is employed by law enforcement and intelligence agencies in which suspects are subjected to psychological pressure in order to elicit information. While this practice has been shown to be effective in some cases, it is also considered unethical by many.

4. Mind control

This is perhaps the most extreme example of dark psychology, in which an individual or group seeks to control another. Often you might see this in the case of cult leaders, who are enigmatic enough to convince their followers to do their every bidding.

CHAPTER 3

THE DARK PSYCHOLOGY TRIAD

The dark psychology triad is a group of three personality traits often associated with people who exhibit apathy, manipulation, and lack of sympathy or empathy.

While all three traits are frequently encountered in one individual, they can also exist independently of one another. Therefore, people with all three characteristics are at risk and must be kept away from.

Characteristics

The theory of the dark triad recognizes specific characteristics associated with each personality trait.

Narcissism

Narcissism is a personality disorder characterized by an inflated sense of self-importance and a preoccupation with oneself. Narcissistic people tend to view others merely as extensions of themselves, and they may be overly focused on their achievements or appearance. In addition, they often have unrealistic expectations of others, demanding that everyone devote their attention to them and recognize their worth at all times.

While narcissism can be a serious issue, most people possess certain narcissistic traits—after all, believing in one's own abilities and celebrating one's own successes is perfectly healthy. However, those who struggle with toxic levels of narcissism may need professional help to work through these issues.

Machiavellianism

Machiavellianism refers to a set of personality traits believed to be associated with manipulative and deceptive behaviors, as well as reverse psychology concepts.

According to the psychoanalytic perspective, Machiavellianism can be thought of as a defense mechanism used by individuals who feel insecure or vulnerable. They use these manipulative behaviors to protect themselves from perceived threats or attacks. However, from a more modern perspective, Machiavellianism is seen as a largely determined set of personality characteristics that arise from a combination of biological factors and social experience.

Regardless of its origin, studies have shown that Machiavellianism is often linked to adverse outcomes such as anger, distrust, and strife within social relationships. Thus, while it may not be possible to eliminate this trait's influence on our behavior, we can still take steps to minimize its harmful effects on our lives.

Psychopathy

Psychopathy is a mental disorder characterized by a lack of empathy and remorse, as well as anti-social behaviors such as manipulation and deceit. Individuals with psychopathy often have a high degree of charm and charisma, which can draw people in and make them easy targets.

While psychopathy is often associated with violent behavior, not all psychopaths are criminals. Some may function relatively well in society, although they may still struggle with personal relationships. Psychopathy is believed to be caused by a combination of genetic factors and early childhood experiences. There is no cure for psychopathy, but some treatments may help manage its symptoms.

Causes, Effects and Correlations

The dark-triad personality traits are consistently found to be more prominent in men than in women. Some researchers have pointed to cultural constructs of masculinity and femininity, and more specifically to negative sexist stereotypes, as a source of dark-triad traits in men. Many researchers have explored how dark-triad traits are tied to other forms of prejudice, such as racism. One study suggested that narcissists and psychopaths are generally anti-social while Machiavellians are biased against racial out-groups. Another found a correlation between dark personality traits and a social-dominance outlook (that is, an attitude of acceptance toward social hierarchies).

Psychologists have found a genetic or hereditary component to each of the dark-triad personalities, though the component is much more significant for psychopathy and narcissism than for Machiavellianism. Environmental factors and formative experiences are also thought to play roles in developing these personality traits.

Because dark-triad personality traits occur at subclinical levels, people with variable tendencies for these traits can live normal lives. Studies show, however, that they often face negative consequences at work and in personal relationships. One study, for example, found that in love relationships dark-triad traits correlate with frequent and more-hostile disagreements. Dark-triad traits are also found to correlate with toxic work behaviours such as manipulation and forceful tactics of influence. Additionally, psychologists report a dark-triad correlation with counterproductive workplace behaviours such as taking shortcuts on tasks.

Who uses Dark Psychology and Manipulation tactics?

Dark psychology and manipulation tactics are often used by people in positions of power to control those around them.

- For example, a politician could employ dark psychological techniques to influence the media to present clear images of them.
- A salesperson employs manipulative tactics to convince customers to purchase products they don't need.
- A boss could employ psychological tricks to control employees and ensure they are in line.

These are all examples of individuals who might use dark psychology strategies, but it is essential to remember that anyone could be the target of these tactics.

While many people consider dark psychology and manipulation illegal, some professions utilize these techniques to their advantage. For instance, law enforcement officers typically utilize dark psychology to collect information on criminals. In addition, psychologists also utilize dark psychology to study how the mind works and help individuals overcome difficulties.

Anyone can benefit from knowing more about the darker side of psychological research. If you know how these methods operate, you'll be better able to defend yourself from these tactics. In addition, if you ever encounter a situation where you're required to employ these strategies, you can ensure that you're doing it correctly.

How to use Dark Psychology?

Different strategies are more or less effective based on the circumstance. For example, specific manipulations or mind games might be more appropriate for specific objectives. A few basic strategies are using personal triggers to influence the target or playing with their fears and anxieties to lower their confidence and effectiveness.

Understanding the dynamics of dark psychology allows you to manipulate other people more effectively and leverage their weaknesses to defeat them.

In Social Interactions

In its essence, dark psychology is the dark side of human nature. This includes manipulative, deceitful, and guilt-tripping. These behaviors manifest in a variety of ways in interactions with others. Some, for instance, employ devious tactics or strategies to derail their opponents in a professional setting. Or, a person might be hyper-aggressive or angry in a dispute with a spouse or family member.

In Dating

There are many ways to utilize the concepts of dark psychology - be it through denial of love, gaslighting, deceit, or any other tactic. The primary objective is to obtain what you want from your love relationships. A method that can help you develop an impression of power and control of your subject is to control their feelings.

For example, you could make fun of their fears by flirting while saying they might lose their lover anytime. On the other hand, you can also capitalize on their desire to be socially validated by lavishly applauding them and not focusing on their flaws, a practice known as the love bomb. Whatever way you choose to go about this, the dark side of psychology offers an array of effective methods to gain advantages in your dating life.

In Business and the Workplace

Perhaps the most common use is in marketing and sales, where the ability to manipulate individuals' emotional reactions can give an edge in competitive environments.

Using persuasive language and emotional appeals to evoke responses such as fear, disgust, or even arousal can help a company stand out from its competitors and increase sales. In addition to marketing and sales, dark psychology can also be used strategically in workplace governance. This includes things like persuasion and negotiation tactics that can be used to gain subliminal influence over others effectively without resorting to unscrupulous means.

In Politics

Dark psychology has been used in politics for centuries, and its use is constantly rising. There are many ways to use dark psychology in politics, but some of the most common uses include playing on fears, exploiting vulnerabilities, brainwashing, and creating divisions. Dark psychology can be used to manipulate people's emotions and get them to act against their best interests.

Politicians who use dark psychology are often skilled at creating an "us vs. them" mentality, leading to division and conflict. They may also try to play on people's fears or exploit their vulnerabilities to get them to vote for them or support their policies. While dark psychology can be used for good or evil, it is often used in politics to gain power or advantage over others.

In Wartime

When fighting, countries employ all the tools they have to be victorious. That includes the use of psychological warfare and propaganda and other strategies to increase the opponent's motivation and willingness to fight. One method of doing this is through the dark side of psychology and by targeting mental triggers which motivate individuals to engage in destructive or self-destructive actions.

Through understanding the dark side of psychology, countries can develop strategies that undermine their adversaries' capability to operate as a combat force. For example, they may communicate incorrect information, leading to the enemy making poor choices or targeting individuals with messages that undermine morale. Lastly, dark psychology can be an effective weapon in battle, which should not be ignored.

Dangers of using Dark Psychology

While some might say that the practice is illegal, others believe there is no harm in using dark psychology for their advantage. However, they fail to recognize that dark psychology is a risky activity with numerous risks, ranging from psychological and manipulative behavior to theft of identities and physical crime.

One of the most threatening risks associated with dark psychology is the potential to influence individuals to commit violent crimes or even murder. People who employ techniques of dark psychology like gaslighting or social conditioning can be enthralled by their new confidence and may be tempted to think they are superior to others. Because they aren't concerned about the feelings of others or their well-being, they might begin to engage in violent or even criminal acts to control other people.

Additionally, even small actions of exploitation could get out of hand, leading their creators into a dangerous direction of extreme cruelty and an inability to feel regret.

While dark psychology can be beneficial in the short term, its long-term effects could be highly damaging. Therefore, if we're going to employ darkness psychology in whatever way, we must be cautious when using the technique and understand that there are always risks involved..

How do people use dark psychology?

Many practitioners of dark psychology use it to gain power for personal or professional gain. Given below are 5 common techniques.

1. Gaining trust through love bombing

Love bombing is a form of psychological manipulation in which an individual deliberately uses flattery, gifts, and attention to gain control over another person. Although it is often used in relationships, it can also occur in friendships, family relationships, and work environments. Love bombers typically display excessive amounts of affection and attention early on in the relationship in order to create an intense bond. They may also make grand promises or give lavish gifts in order to further their control. Over time, the love bomber may begin to withdraw their support and instead use criticism, and emotional control to maintain power.

2. Gaslighting

Gaslighting is a form of emotional abuse in which the abuser deliberately tries to undermine the victim's sense of reality. It is an insidious form of control that can have a devastating effect on the victim's mental health. Gaslighting usually starts gradually, with the abuser making small changes to the victim's environment or routine. The aim is to create confusion and doubt in the victim's mind so that they second-guess their own memories and perceptions. Over time, the victim may start to doubt their own sanity. If you suspect that you're being exposed to these techniques, it is important to seek help from a trusted friend or professional.

3. Passive-aggressive behavior

Passive-aggressive psychological manipulation is a type of emotional manipulation that can be difficult to spot because it often masquerades as normal behavior. Passive-aggressive manipulators may seem withdrawn or uninterested, but in reality, they are carefully monitoring your reaction to their behavior. They may withhold information or make unpleasant comments in an attempt to get you to react. If you suspect that someone is trying to manipulate you emotionally, it is essential to pay attention to your gut feelings and take steps to protect yourself. You may need to set boundaries or build a support network of people you can trust. Remember, you are not responsible for the manipulator's happiness, and you should not let them control your emotions.

4. Emotional blackmail

Emotional blackmail is a powerful psychological manipulation tool that can be used to control and exploit others. It usually involves the threat of withholding love unless the victim complies with the blackmailer's demands. Often, emotional blackmailers will use guilt or fear to induce their victims to do what they want. For example, a parent might threaten to withdraw their love if their child does not obey them, causing damage to relationships and emotional distress.

5. Withdrawing affection

One common manipulation tactic is withdrawing affection, which often accompanies emotional blackmail. This can take many forms, from refusing to speak to someone to withholding physical affection, and it is often used in order to punish someone or force them into doing something. Withdrawing affection can be an incredibly powerful tool, as it taps into our deep-seated need for connection and approval. When we're cut off from those things, it can cause us a great deal of distress. In some cases, the pain of being disconnected from another person can be enough to motivate them to change their behavior.

CHAPTER 4

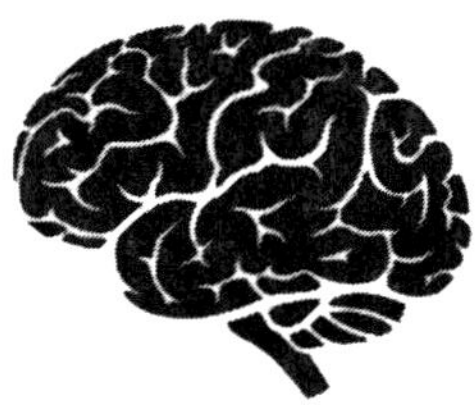

EFFECTS AND IMPACT OF DARK PSYCHOLOGY

Dark psychology is about understanding and exploiting the weaknesses of human psychology. By understanding how people think and feel, practitioners of dark psychology can easily manipulate others into doing what they want. This can be used for any number of purposes, from getting someone to buy a product they don't need to convincing them to commit a crime.

While dark psychology can be used for nefarious purposes, some use it for more positive ends. For example, therapists may use dark psychology techniques to help patients overcome their fears and phobias. In other cases, police officers can use dark psychology tricks to get confessions from criminals.

How can you protect yourself from the dangers of Dark Psychology?

Dark psychology can be used for both good and evil. But how can you protect yourself from its dangers?

The first step is to educate yourself about the topic. Learn about the different techniques used in dark psychology and how to spot them. This will help you be more aware of what is happening around you and enable you to better protect yourself from being manipulated or deceived.

Secondly, surround yourself with people who have your best interests at heart. These people will be less likely to take advantage of you and help you stay safe in an increasingly dangerous world.

Finally, trust your gut instinct. If something feels wrong, it probably is. Don't be afraid to walk away from a situation that makes you uncomfortable or uneasy.

Can people be cured of their tendencies towards Dark Psychology?

There is much debate surrounding the concept of dark psychology and whether or not people can be cured of their tendencies toward it.

Some experts believe that dark psychology is simply a result of learned behaviors and that with the right therapy, people can unlearn these behaviors. However, others believe that dark psychology is more inherent and that people are born with certain predispositions that cannot be changed.

There is still much research to be done in this area, but it seems that there is no simple answer as to whether or not people can be cured of dark tendencies in social circumstances.

CHAPTER 5

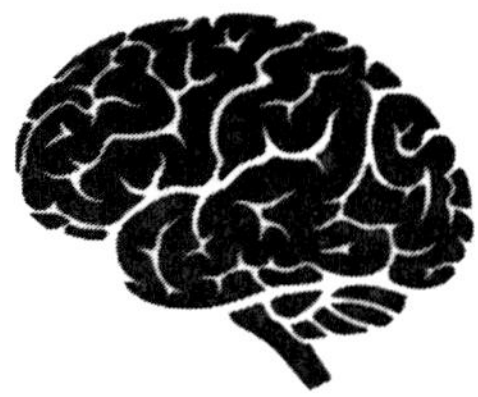

DARK PSYCHOLOGY: MANIPULATION AND MIND CONTROL

Dark psychology is the science of mind control and manipulation. If psychology refers to the study of the behavior of humans and focuses on actions, interactions, and thoughts, dark psychology is a phenomenon where people use tactics of coercion, manipulation, persuasion, and motivation just to get the things they want.

Psychologists and criminologists identify "The Dark Triad" as the easy way of predicting not only criminal behavior but also broken and problematic relationships.

The traits included in the Dark Triad are:

Machiavellianism - The use of manipulation to exploit and deceive people with no sense of morality.

Narcissism - It involves lack of empathy, grandiosity and egotism.

Psychopathy - Usually friendly and charming but is characterized by remorselessness, lack of empathy, impulsivity, and selfishness.

No one wants to be manipulated but the sad news is that it can happen pretty often. You might not be the subject to a person who belongs to Dark Triad. However, average people encounter tactics of dark psychology every single day.

These strategies can often be seen in online ads, commercials, sales methods, and even the behaviors of superiors at work. Parents of kids, specifically teens, will most definitely experience such tactics as their children start experimenting with behaviors to seek autonomy and get the things they want. Manipulation and mind control are the issues that interest young learners mostly these days. The truth is that dark persuasion and covert manipulation are typically used by those people that you love and trust.

Some of the most common tactics that normal everyday people use include the following:

- Lying – Untrue stories, partial truths, exaggeration, and untruths

- Love flooding – Affection, buttering a person to make a request, and compliments
- Withdrawal – Silent treatment or avoiding a person
- Love denial – Withhold affection and attention
- Reverse psychology – Tell a person to do something or another with the purpose of motivating them to do the exact opposite which is what you really want.
- Choice restricting – Offering specific choices that will distract from the option that you wouldn't want the person to make.
- Semantic manipulation – The use of words believed to have a mutual or common definition but the manipulator will later tell you that they have a different understanding or definition of the conversation.

While there are people who use dark psychology tactics know what they are really doing and their intention is to manipulate others to get what they want, there are also those who use unethical and dark tactics unknowingly.

Many of them have learned these tactics from their parents when they were still young. There are also those who mastered the tactics during their adulthood or teenage years by chance. They tried a manipulation tactic by accident and this worked. As a result, they continued using tactics to help them in getting their way all the time.

Dark psychology is pretty much a part of people's everyday lives. With the things mentioned above, you will see how easy it is for you to fall for these tactics. Either you are the victim or the perpetrator.

Managing your Modes of Manipulation

When most people think of a brainwashed individual, they imagine someone whose mind is completely controlled. Some evil but powerful authority is manipulating his or her will. In the most extreme cases — as when a cult leader instructs his followers to commit suicide — or when an oppressive political regime demands unquestionable obedience and adoration — this does seem to be true. Yet the human tendency to manipulate others, as well as to be manipulated, is far more common that these rare extremes would suggest.

Most of us first get acquainted with psychological manipulation at a young age. The school bully, for example, is a young master manipulator who has learned early on how to use intimidation to get what he or she wants. Researchers have found that the brains of bullies exhibit a pleasure response at the sight of other's pain, rendering them addicted to the experience of being cruel to others, and that the brain development of their victims can be permanently stunted by the abuse.

A group of researches in the **British Journal of Developmental Psychology** theorizes that most often bullying arises in certain children who, contrary to common assumptions, have highly developed social skills. Typically, these kids tend to lack social standing — perhaps due to poor academic performance or low economic status — but have learned to cultivate social power in their own ways. They are well versed in the art of psychological manipulation, the ability to influence people by underhanded, deceptive, and abusive means. Although bullies may be less subtle than adult manipulators, they exploit one human frailty that all manipulators tend to use to their advantage — fear.

Terrorists, for example, can be seen as manipulators of mass psychology. Like bullies, they lack power to influence or destroy their enemy through politics and traditional warfare. Instead, they attempt to implant fear in the mass consciousness of the society or group they oppose.

A destructive cult leader, an icon of manipulation in the minds of most people, also uses fear to control his disciples' minds. The end result of this manipulation sometimes seems mind boggling to those outside of the group in question, as in the 1978 case of the mass suicide of 918 people at Jonestown in Guyana, South America. In this example, the charismatic leader, Jim Jones, instructed his followers to drink cyanide-laced punch because, according to him, war and certain doom were on their way. The vast majority of followers complied; particularly disturbing were the parents who fed their children poison.

Like many cult manipulators, Jones first enticed people into the group by giving them what they wanted — the promise of a paradise free of society's ills — and then turned the tables to create a nightmare of totalistic control. Not only did Jones use every means possible to control his followers personally, he urged his followers to do the same to one another through a culture of mutual spying and tattling. Fear of being shamed by and ostracized from the group led members deeper and deeper into Jones' clutches as they surrendered their individual sense of self-determination to him.

As extreme as that situation might seem, it is not that different from certain elements of the socialization process that encourage all of us to conform. Parents, peers, and other authority figures often use manipulation to ensure that we become who they want us to be, especially as we are growing up. For instance, boys who naturally exhibit feminine characteristics are often shamed and ostracized by parents and peers until they develop more masculine behavior. Even relatively benign parenting techniques employ manipulation, such as when a parent tells a child that Santa won't bring presents to naughty children. It's a lie, but it works to get kids in line during the busy holiday season.

In our consumer culture, manipulative techniques are widely used to get us to buy more — far more than we require for survival. Advertising, which pervades almost every aspect of Western culture, is more likely to use manipulation to sell a product than straight facts. Most ads, whether print, TV, or online, prey on our emotional and psychological needs, such as the need to fit in and feel good about ourselves. A juice commercial, for example, is more likely to suggest "Good parents buy their kids this product" than to provide concrete information about its nutritional benefits. Like other forms of manipulation, these ads are effective because of our deeply held fears, such as being a poor parent, being victimized, becoming a social outcast and being thought of as unattractive.

Inevitably, manipulation is all around us, from the emotional manipulation that influences our relationships to the unspoken cultural messages that prompt us to behave in a certain manner. There may be no way to eliminate its effects from our daily lives, but awareness of how we experience it — and how we use it on others — might be the first step toward using our brains in better ways.

Behavioral and Character Traits of the Manipulators

- Manipulators have identifiable behavioral and character traits, such as lying by commission and omission, which involve purposefully telling someone something with the intention of deceiving them or leaving out certain details, as well as failing to correct misconceptions.

- Manipulators use techniques such as lying by omission and denial to deceive and confuse people into believing false conclusions that benefit them, while psychopaths use denial to deceive both themselves and others, indicating a lack of conscious and an unwillingness to change.
- Manipulative people use denial, rationalization, and minimization as tactics to avoid taking responsibility and to manage the way others perceive them.
- Manipulators use minimization to belittle or discount achievements, make emotions seem insignificant, and make it seem as though their actions aren't as harmful as they are. They also use diversion and evasion to avoid taking responsibility for their actions.
- Evasion and diversion are techniques used to avoid giving a straight answer to a question and involve changing the topic or steering the conversation in a different direction. Covert intimidation and guilt tripping use the same underlying principle, preying on a person's emotions, and are used by people with covert-aggressive personalities.
- Manipulators can use guilt tripping and shaming to control and exploit people by making them feel guilty or ashamed for their actions, or by threatening to reveal secrets.
- Manipulators use tactics such as shaming, vilifying the victim, and playing the victim or servant role to control and deceive their victims.
- Manipulators use a variety of tactics such as playing the victim, playing the servant, and seduction to gain power and control over their victims.

- Manipulators use tactics such as projecting blame and brandishing anger to control and manipulate their victims.
- Manipulative people use anger to convey fake moral outrage, intimidate others, and make themselves feel superior.

What is Covert Emotional Manipulation?

Covert emotional manipulation is a form of power and control used by people to alter the way someone thinks and behaves without them being aware of it, resulting in a loss of self-esteem and identity.

Emotional manipulation in relationships can take the form of positive reinforcement, negative reinforcement, false intimacy, and well-calculated insinuations in order to control and dominate the other person.

Friends can manipulate others through passive aggression, silent treatment, subtle insults, and power trips in order to control social interactions and gain emotional reliance.

Colleagues can manipulate others by using emotional manipulation, favors, leaving out of the loop, and using dark personality traits to gain an advantage.

What are Manipulators trying to do?

Manipulators have a psychological need to control others, and seek to weaken their victims in order to gain dominance by cancelling their willpower, destroying their self-esteem, seeking passive-aggressive revenge, or confusing their reality.

Manipulative people can deplete one's willpower and destroy one's self-esteem by using carefully worded phrases, blaming them for all sorts of problems, giving them looks that say everything, flooding them with negative information, neglecting them emotionally, and feeding their fears.

Manipulative people seek to gain power over their victims by exploiting their low self-esteem, while passive-aggressive people may target their victims for revenge, even if the victim has done nothing wrong.

Manipulators seek passive-aggressive revenge against their victims by using disguised verbal hostility, invalidating their thoughts and feelings, and attempting to confuse their reality in order to gain control over them.

Narcissists and bullies/sadists attempt to confuse others' reality in order to impose their own delusions of grandeur or pessimistic outlook.

Behavioral Traits of Favorite Victims of Manipulators

Manipulators tend to target victims who are emotionally insecure or fragile, have social anxiety, or are emotionally fragile due to a difficult situation, as well as highly sensitive people who are more aware of subtleties in social dynamics.

Manipulators target sensitive and empathetic people because they are easy to exploit due to their heightened emotions, politeness, and generosity.

Emphatic people are often taken advantage of by malicious people due to their fear of loneliness, abandonment issues, and fear of disappointing others.

People with dependent personality disorder and emotional dependency are easy targets for manipulators, as they are willing to cede control over their lives and are often driven by a fear of disappointing others or losing their partners.

CHAPTER 6

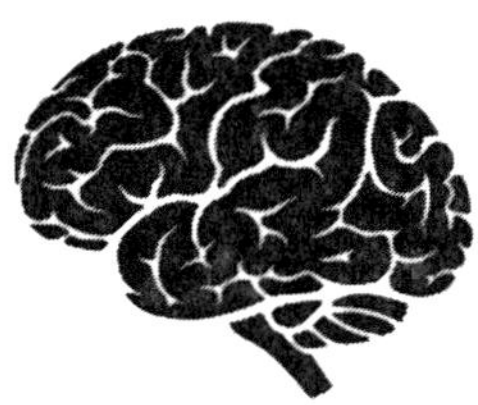

DECEPTION

Deception refers to the act—big or small, cruel or kind—of encouraging people to believe information that is not true. Lying is a common form of deception—stating something known to be untrue with the intent to deceive.

While most people are generally honest, even those who subscribe to honesty engage in deception sometimes. Studies show that the average person lies several times a day. Some of those lies are big ("I've never cheated on you!") but more often, they are little white lies ("That dress looks fine") deployed to avoid uncomfortable situations or spare someone's feelings.

Trust is the bedrock of social life at all levels, from love and parenting to national government. Deception always undermines it. Because truth is so essential to the human enterprise, which relies on a shared view of reality, the default assumption most people have is that others are truthful in their communications and dealings. Most cultures have powerful social sanctions against lying.

The Many Forms of Deception

There are sins of commission and sins of omission; omitting information and concealing the truth are considered lies when they are done with an intent to deceive. In addition to statements that are false, deception encompasses statements that misrepresent or distort facts as well as the withholding of information. People can lie through outright statements or by strategic silence.

What kinds of lies do people tell?

People may deliberately create false information or fabricate a story. But most often, sheer invention is not the soul of lying. Rather, people deceive by omitting information, denying the truth, or exaggerating information. Or they might agree with others when in fact they don't, in order to preserve a relationship. Self-serving lies, on the other hand, help liars get what they want, make them look better, or spare them blame or embarrassment.

How do I lie to myself?

Deception isn't always an outward-facing act. There are also the lies people tell themselves, for reasons ranging from maintenance of self-esteem to serious delusions beyond their control. While lying to oneself is generally perceived as harmful, some experts argue that certain kinds of self-deception—like believing one can accomplish a difficult goal even if evidence exists to the contrary—can have a positive effect on overall well-being.

How to spot Deception?

Researchers have long searched for ways to definitively detect when someone is lying. They know that some people are better at lying than others; their visual and verbal cues are in sync with what they are saying. But studies consistently show that most people are terrible at detecting deception, performing no better than chance. There's evidence that many people have inaccurate beliefs about signals of lying—for example, that fidgeting is always a giveaway.

How do I know when I'm being lied to?

Many experts propose that liars reveal themselves in "tells," major and minor changes in body language or facial expressions. But observable signs of lying can be unreliable. Researchers do find that some people lie more than others. Studies show that children under two never lie and that lying peaks in adolescence, when social relationships take on a heightened importance.

How do I know when I'm lying to myself?

Most people are not aware of the ways they fool themselves. But psychologist have identified many signals of self-deception. Outsize emotional reactions to present situations, behavior that is out of step with who you claim or aim to be can be indicators that we believe things about ourselves that are false or fail to believe things that are true.

Why people engage in Deception?

According to one expert, lies are like wishes—often, what is said are things people wish were true. A large body of research identifies three major reasons why people lie: to get something they want, so-called instrumental reasons; to protect or promote themselves; and to harm others. Avoiding punishment may be the main motivation for both children and adults.

While everyone lies a little, it appears that only a small percentage of people do most of the lying. There's evidence that prolific liars share the personality trait of Machiavellianism: They are manipulative and exploitative of others; the trait is closely related to psychopathy.

Is honesty always the best policy?

Intentions matter when it comes to behavior—it's often a deciding factor in the law—and there are times when lies can help others or shield them from harm. Sometimes lies are told to prevent difficult conversations, such as those involving critical feedback, and they may appear protective. But they can ultimately disadvantage the recipient by depriving him or her of useful information that can promote positive change.

Is Deception always harmful?

Experts differ on the topic. Some believe that even white lies, told with the aim of protecting others or smoothing social relationships, are damaging because they deny people the experience of reality that could be used to improve their lives. Lies are damaging to relationships because they block intimacy. Lies are considered harmful because they destroy trust—the bedrock of society—the belief that others are dependable and intend no harm.

The Ethics of Deception

Psychologists operate under rules that ensure they are taking into account ethical considerations. Because deception could cause harm to participants the use of deception in research is spelled out in their ethical guidelines. The APA ethics code states that a psychologist should not use deception unless the ends justify the means. Therefore, deception can be used if the outcome of the study outweighs the potential harm of deceptive tactics. It is difficult to make the argument the outcome of research is so valuable that it justifies the use of deception. Further, if any deception is used, it must be revealed as soon as feasibly possible in the experimental process.

Types of Deception

Deception falls under two types: direct or indirect.

Direct deception

Direct deception is when participants are deliberately provided with misinformation about an experiment, including false instructions, staged situations, intentionally misleading feedback, or the use of exaggerations and minimizations.

Indirect deception

Indirect deception occurs when participants agree to postpone full disclosure of the true purpose of the research or when the goals of the study are not conveyed to the participant to mislead them.

Advantages and Disadvantages of Deception

These are the pros and cons of using deception in research:

Advantages

Deception allows researchers to obtain information they would normally be unable to find in a natural setting. For example, an experiment could create an "emergency" situation using confederates that allows researchers to measure people's reactions to that certain circumstance.

Deception in research provides the opportunity for real reactions to be measured. If people are unaware of the goals of a study you are more likely to get an authentic response from participants, rather than subjects reacting how they believe they are supposed to behave.

Disadvantages

Deception can lead to suspicion among participants, causing them to behave in a way that they normally would not.

Deception takes advantage of the trust of participants and creates a bad reputation for psychological research. As a result, it can leave the subject pool biased by making it less likely that certain people will want to participate.

It can be argued that a participant, in order to give informed consent, must know the true objectives of a research study. It is a matter of maintaining experimental integrity. For these reasons, some may argue that any deception is unethical.

Examples of Deception in Psychological Research

Milgram's Obedience Experiment (1963)

Stanley Milgram conducted an experiment to measure an individual's obedience to instructions from an authority figure. Participants were asked to deliver electric shocks to people they thought were fellow research subjects (they were really confederates). Of course, having participants falsely believe they were inflicting pain on others is a major form of deception and would not be allowed today. Even for the time, it was ethically questionable. However, its findings lent an understanding as to the reason why Germans committed the atrocities of WWII.

The Robbers Cave Experiment (1954)

The goal of Muzafer Sherif's experiment was to see how a group of fifth-grade boys handled intergroup conflict. Sherif and his team brought two groups of boys to a summer camp setting and then proceeded to introduce variables to pit the two groups against each other before attempting to bring them together with a task in which they were forced to work together. The whole experiment was deceptive; the boys believed they were attending summer camp, not participating in a social experiment on group dynamics. To begin with, trying to invite conflict between unknowing groups of people is of questionable ethics. The fact that the subjects were fifth graders makes it even more controversial. Although the experiment exhibited the power of inter-group social dynamics, its manipulation of children lent ammunition to critics of the use of deception.

Brown Eyes vs. Blue Eyes Experiment (1968)

Jane Elliot was not a psychologist. She was a third-grade teacher in rural Iowa. In the aftermath of the Martin Luther King assassination, she wanted to teach her students what discrimination felt like. So, without letting her students know she performed an experiment. She told them that their eye color determined if one was better than the other. On the first day, blue-eyed children were told they were smarter, cleaner, and nicer. She then proceeded to treat the blue-eyed children better than the brown-eyed kids. The next day she reversed the experiment. What she found was that the children's emotions and behavior reflected their status within the classroom. Although this was a valuable result, such manipulation of a third grader's feelings would not be allowed today.

Bystander Effect Experiment (1968)

In the aftermath of the Kitty Genovese killing, there arose considerable interest in the social construct of bystander apathy. Psychologists Bibb Latané and John Darley wanted to find out more about why people did not call for help when someone else was experiencing an emergency. They created an experiment where they made participants believe that someone in the next room was having an epileptic fit to gauge their response. They found that people are much more likely to respond when they were alone compared to when other people are around. This introduced the concept of "diffusion of responsibility." Although this was an important concept in social psychology, the distress it may have caused participants would make it untenable today.

The Asch Conformity Experiment (1951)

The Asch experiment is a good example of the use of deception where the harm experienced by the participants was minimal. Solomon Asch wanted to study how group social pressure affected conformity. He asked people to match the length of line segments with others of a similar size. Subjects were almost 100 percent accurate when matching the length of the line alone. He then had confederates disagree with the participants' judgments. He found that approximately one-third of subjects then said they agreed with confederates even though the confederates were wrong, thus exhibiting the impact of social pressure. Although deception was used in this experiment, the value of the conclusions appears to outweigh the level of harm experienced by participants.

The Psychological Impact of Deception

Speaking of harm, what is the impact of deception? As we have already discussed, it may dissuade people from participating in psychological research and suspicion may invalidate results. But, does it actually hurt people? Experiments such as the **Tuskegee Syphilis Study**, where subjects were withheld treatment that could have saved their lives, are a remnant of the early 20th century and do not apply to current studies.

Like almost any issue, there is more than one opinion. There is some evidence that points to deception causing resentment and other negative emotions. **Michael Cheng-TekTai** argues that deception in research is never ethical and should not be permitted

However, **Allan Kimmel** notes that some studies have shown that people who participate in deception experiments "report having enjoyed deception experiments more and receiving more educational benefit from them." Other researchers conclude that minimal types of deception, such as false feedback or masking the hypothesis of a study, cause little psychological harm to participants.

Deceptive research in psychology has decreased since the 20th century but it has not entirely disappeared. The ethical guidelines surrounding its use are relatively strict and have been effective in reducing risk to participants. It has been noted that a basic debriefing procedure is likely effective in counteracting the consequences of deception as currently used. Because of its advantages and minimal risk, deception continues to be used for scientific gain.

CHAPTER 7

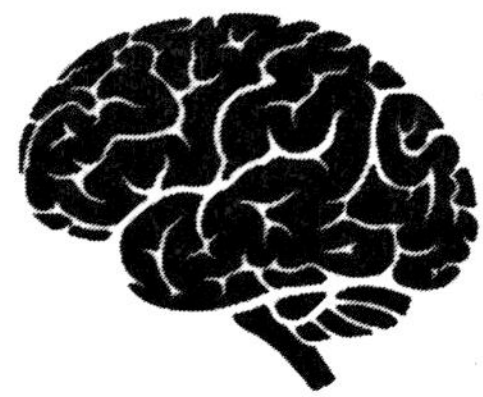

HYPNOSIS

Hypnosis is a state of heightened focus and concentration used to help individuals gain control over undesirable behaviors, cope with anxiety and pain, and manage side effects of cancer treatment.

The use of hypnotic-like trance states dates back thousands of years, but hypnosis began to grow during the late 18th-century from the work of a physician named **Franz Mesmer.**

Hypnotism became more important in the field of psychology in the late 19th-century and was used by **Jean-**

Martin Charcot to treat women experiencing what was then known as hysteria. This work influenced Sigmund Freud and the development of psychoanalysis.

More recently, there have been a number of different theories to explain exactly how hypnosis works. One of the best-known theories is **Hilgard's neo-dissociation theory of hypnosis.**

According to Hilgard, people in a hypnotic state experience a split consciousness in which there are two different streams of mental activity. While one stream of consciousness responds to the hypnotist's suggestions, another dissociated stream processes information outside of the hypnotized individual's conscious awareness.

Hypnosis is a trance-like mental state in which people experience increased attention, concentration, and suggestibility. While hypnosis is often described as a sleep-like state, it is better expressed as a state of focused attention, heightened suggestibility, and vivid fantasies.

People in a hypnotic state often seem sleepy and zoned out, but in reality, they are in a state of hyper-awareness.

While there are many myths and misconceptions, hypnosis is a very real process that can be used as a therapeutic tool. Hypnosis has been shown to have medical and therapeutic benefits, most notably in the reduction of pain and anxiety. It has even been suggested that hypnosis can reduce the symptoms of dementia.

Hypnosis is a therapeutic technique used to induce a trance-like state in which a person is more open to suggestion and can access their subconscious mind, which is divided into three stages: Hypnoidal state, Cataleptic state, and Somnambulistic state. It is used to treat a variety of conditions, such as phobias, smoking cessation, weight loss, and boosting confidence. It is also used in anesthesiology during surgery.

Hypnotherapy is a form of therapy that uses hypnosis to align the subconscious and conscious mind, and is used to treat a variety of conditions, such as anxiety and phobias, through the use of cognitive, Ericksonian, hypno-psychotherapy, hypnoanalysis, NLP, past life regression, solution-focused, and suggestion techniques.

Types of Hypnosis

There are different ways that hypnosis can be delivered:

Guided hypnosis: This form of hypnosis involves the use of tools such as recorded instructions and music to induce a hypnotic state. Online sites and mobile apps often utilize this form of hypnosis.

Hypnotherapy: Hypnotherapy is the use of hypnosis in psychotherapy and is practiced by licensed physicians and psychologists to treat conditions including depression, anxiety, post-traumatic stress disorder (PTSD), and eating disorders.

Self-hypnosis: Self-hypnosis is a process that occurs when a person self-induces a hypnotic state. It is often used as a self-help tool for controlling pain or managing stress.

Uses and Potential Benefits

Why does a person decide to try hypnosis? In some cases, people might seek out hypnosis to help deal with chronic pain or to alleviate pain and anxiety caused by medical procedures such as surgery or childbirth.

The following are a few applications for hypnosis that have been demonstrated through research:

- Alleviation of symptoms associated with irritable bowel syndrome (IBS)
- Control of pain during dental procedures
- Elimination or reduction of skin conditions including warts and psoriasis
- Management of certain symptoms of ADHD
- Treatment of chronic pain conditions such as rheumatoid arthritis
- Treatment and reduction of pain during childbirth
- Reduction of dementia symptoms
- Reduction of nausea and vomiting in cancer patients undergoing chemotherapy

Hypnosis has also been used to help people with behavior changes such as quitting smoking, losing weight, or preventing bed-wetting.

Impact of Hypnosis

The experience of hypnosis can vary dramatically from one person to another.

Some hypnotized individuals report feeling a sense of detachment or extreme relaxation during the hypnotic state while others even feel that their actions seem to occur outside of their conscious volition. Other individuals may remain fully aware and able to carry out conversations while under hypnosis.

Experiments by researcher Ernest Hilgard demonstrated how hypnosis can be used to dramatically alter perceptions. After instructing a hypnotized individual not to feel pain in their arm, the participant's arm was then placed in ice water. While non-hypnotized individuals had to remove their arm from the water after a few seconds due to the pain, the hypnotized individuals were able to leave their arms in the icy water for several minutes without experiencing pain.

Tips for Hypnosis

While many people think that they cannot be hypnotized, research has shown that a large number of people are more hypnotizable than they believe. Research suggests that:

- Between 10% to 15% of people are very responsive to hypnosis.
- Approximately 10% of adults are considered difficult or impossible to hypnotize.
- Children tend to be more susceptible to hypnosis.
- People who can become easily absorbed in fantasies are much more responsive to hypnosis.

If you are interested in being hypnotized, it is important to remember to approach the experience with an open mind. People who view hypnosis in a positive light tend to respond better.

If you are interested in trying hypnotherapy, it is important to look for a professional who has credentials and experience in the use of hypnosis as a therapeutic tool.

While there are many places that offer hypnosis training and certification, it may be helpful to look for a mental health professional who has been certified by the American Society of Clinical Hypnosis. Their program is open to health professionals with a master's degree and requires 40 hours of approved workshop training, 20 hours of individual training, and two years of practice in clinical hypnosis.

Potential Pitfalls

Misunderstandings about hypnosis are common.

- While amnesia may occur in very rare cases, people generally remember everything that transpired while they were hypnotized. However, hypnosis can have a significant effect on memory. Posthypnotic amnesia can lead an individual to forget certain things that occurred before or during hypnosis. However, this effect is generally limited and temporary.

- While hypnosis can be used to enhance memory, the effects have been dramatically exaggerated in popular media. Research has found that hypnosis does not lead to significant memory enhancement or accuracy, and hypnosis can actually result in false or distorted memories.

- Despite stories about people being hypnotized without their consent, hypnosis does require voluntary participation on the part of the patient. People do vary in terms of how hypnotizable and suggestible they are while under hypnosis, however. Research suggests that people who are highly suggestible are more likely to experience a reduced sense of agency while under hypnosis.

- While people often feel that their actions under hypnosis seem to occur without the influence of their will, a hypnotist cannot make you perform actions that are against your wishes.

- While hypnosis can be used to enhance performance, it cannot make people stronger or more athletic than their existing physical capabilities.

CHAPTER 8

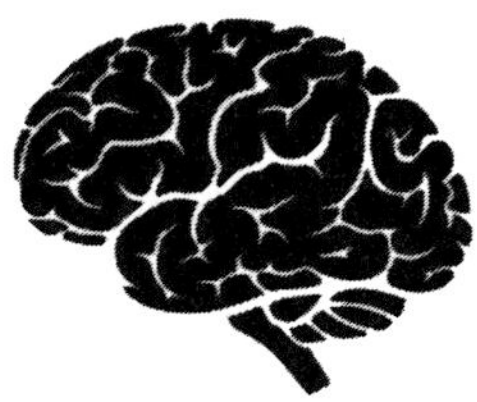

PROBLEM BEHAVIORS

Problem behaviors are continuous behaviors that hinder social relations, communications and learning of a child and cause harm to them, their families, their peers and other adults. Although they show themselves as tantrums, some cases may also show reactions like long sobbing fits. Unless the problem behaviors are eliminated, it would be impossible for the child to complete his development.

Problem behaviors, prevent the child from using his current skills. Children with these behavioral patterns bear the risk of losing their skills because of not putting them into practice. For instance, a child that has the ability to eat with fork and knife show problem behaviors, he will use the fork and knife to make loud noises rather than eat.

Besides preventing children from using their skills, these behavior patterns also prevent them from acquiring new ones. Because children with repetitive problem behavior will not be open to acquire new skills with experience or teaching, their tantrums and other reactions due to the behavior will hinder these.

Tendency to harm is also seen in children with problem behaviors. The child is prone to harm themselves or others close to them and this poses a serious danger. Many children are known to harm themselves by taking harmful behaviors as habits like hitting themselves, throwing them on the ground and have tantrums more than often.

A child that has problem behaviors will naturally not fit into his environment. Repetitive behaviors like screaming often, making noise by hitting objects, trying to hurt people badly affect the child's adaptation to his environment. This creates a major risk in terms of social development of children. Because these repetitive behaviors will prevent children from getting attention from their peers and making friends with them.

Children with problem behaviors may pose a danger for themselves and their environment. These children are highly prone to be harmful. They can hurt their friends, adults, themselves, people they do not know with various objects. They may also feel the need to disturb people constantly.

What are the reasons to Problem Behavior?

Most of the behavior patterns that are called problem behaviors occur during pre-school or school age. This results from the child spending time in a new environment other than usual parent environment and spending time with people for the first time. Many problems may arise in this period and they may cause the child to acquire problem behavior patterns.

The reasons for problem behaviors can be divided into two as school-related and non-school-related factors.

Non-School-Related Factors:

Family Factor: Researches show that problem behaviors are majorly caused by the features of the family. Even though the child is not directly subjected to violence, when the person that the child takes as role model raises his voice of yell, problem behaviors may be caused. It is known that children in family environment where arguments are common have problem behavior patterns.

Other factors due to family include the child being over-disciplined or not disciplined at all. Children may show problem behaviors when they are under a lot of pressure in family environment and suddenly they feel the lack of this pressure in a new environment. The other way around, undisciplined children are known to show problem behavior due to the effect of being in a social environment for the first time.

If physical or psychological violence is in question in family environment, it is impossible for children to not have problem behaviors.

Even though this violence is not towards the child, what he witnesses will affect him and cause him to have problem behaviors. Thus, parents' attitude, features of the family and behaviors shown in this environment may cause the child to have problem behaviors.

Mass Media: Mass media like TV and Internet are extremely influential on children to have problem behaviors. Even a regular advertisement can adversely affect the child or cause him to acquire a wrong behavior as a role model. Also, cartoon characters can be bad role models for children and cause them to develop problem behaviors. It is known that children spending a long time watching cartoons exhibit various problem behaviors.

Devices that have Internet connection or games on them like computers, tablets, phones may also cause problem behaviors in children. Children's interaction with these kinds of devices should be limited and programs, games, or applications they use should be under parents' supervision. Children should be kept away from violent games regardless of their levels and should be guided towards mind developing games.

School-related Factors:

Features of the School: Physical and cultural features of the school can also cause the child to acquire negative, problem behaviors. For instance, if the school is too crowded, classrooms are at overcapacity, physical features are inadequate and such, children going to this school may show problem behaviors. Because children will seek the comfort of their home there, want to go back to home and show reaction to get them out of this environment. When this situation gains continuity, the child will have acquired a problem behavior. Also, the social and cultural features of the school entity have great importance. Children may show problem behavior among a majority that does not carry the same cultural features as their parents.

What are the symptoms of Problem Behavior?

Problem behavior can have many symptoms, such as,:

- abuse of alcohol or drugs

- agitation
- angry, defiant behaviors
- carelessness
- disinterest or withdrawal from daily life
- drug use
- emotional flatness
- excessive, disruptive talking
- hoarding useless objects
- inappropriate behavior
- inflated self-esteem or overconfidence
- obsessive thoughts
- poor judgment
- property damage
- self-injury

Problem behavior can range from the absence of emotions to aggressive emotions.

According to the **Merck Manual**, behavior problems often show themselves in different ways among girls and boys. For example, boys with problem behavior may fight, steal, or deface property. Girls with problem behavior may lie or run away from home. Both are at greater risk for drug and alcohol abuse.

What causes Problem Behavior?

There are multiple causes associated with problem behavior. A psychiatric or medical professional should evaluate a person with problem behavior to determine the cause.

Causes of problem behavior can be a life event or family situation. A person might have a family conflict, struggle with poverty, feel anxious, or have had a death in the family. Aging can also lead to dementia, which affects a person's behavior.

Common conditions related to problem behavior include:

- anxiety disorder
- attention deficit hyperactivity disorder (ADHD)
- bipolar disorder
- conduct disorder
- delirium
- dementia
- depression
- obsessive-compulsive disorder
- oppositional defiant disorder
- postpartum depression
- post-traumatic stress disorder (PTSD)
- psychosis
- schizophrenia
- substance abuse

What are the risk factors for Problem Behavior?

People with chronic and mental health conditions are at greater risk for problem behavior than those who don't have these conditions.

Some problem behaviors have a genetic link. According to the **Merck Manual**, parents with the following problem behaviors are more likely to have children with problem behavior concerns:

- anti-social disorder
- ADHD
- mood disorder
- schizophrenia
- substance abuse

However, people with problem behavior may also come from families with little history of problem behavior.

When do I seek medical help for Problem Behavior?

Problem behavior can be a medical emergency when the behavior includes the following:

- contemplating suicide
- hallucinations or hearing voices
- harming oneself or others
- threats of violence

Make an appointment with your doctor if you or a loved one experience the following symptoms:

- behavior that affects the ability to function in relationships with others, in the workplace, or at school
- criminal behavior
- cruelty to animals

- engaging in intimidating, bullying, or impulsive behaviors
- excessive feelings of isolation
- low interest in school or work
- social withdrawal

People with problem behavior may feel different from others. Some may have emotions they don't understand or can't identify. This can lead to frustration and more problem behavior.

How is Problem Behavior diagnosed?

A doctor or mental health specialist can evaluate problem behaviors. They'll likely start by taking a health history and listening to a description of an adult or child's symptoms. Some questions a doctor may ask include:

- When did this behavior start?
- How long does the behavior last?
- How has the behavior affected those around the person?
- Has the person recently experienced any life changes or transitions that could trigger the behavior?

Doctors can use this information to pinpoint the behavior's possible cause and diagnosis.

How is Problem Behavior treated?

Doctors treat problem behavior by diagnosing its causes. People who are at risk for harming themselves may require an inpatient stay at a hospital for their personal safety.

Additional treatments for problem behavior can include:

- conflict resolution classes
- counseling
- group therapy
- medications
- parenting skills classes

CHAPTER 9

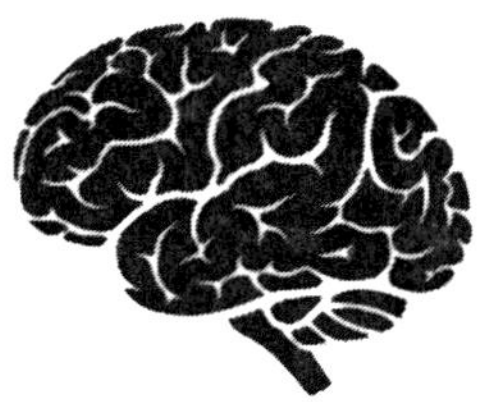

REVERSE PSYCHOLOGY

Reverse psychology is a strategy that many people use to influence a situation to achieve their desired outcome.

When your true intent is different from what you ask a person to do, you are using reverse psychology. The result is that the other person behaves the way you would genuinely like them to, even though you didn't ask them directly.

Psychologists use the term "strategic self-anticonformity" to describe reverse psychology because a person's communicated request is in direct opposition to their actual desire.

Research from 2010 shows that strategic self-anticonformity is an effective method of persuasion that can also generate a sense of reassurance between individuals.

If you're on the receiving end of reverse psychology, you will likely experience a psychological phenomenon known as reactance, which is a strong negative or emotional reaction in opposition to how another person is attempting to influence you. The catch is that you're responding precisely how they wanted you to.

Reverse psychology is a form of manipulation. However, in many cases, the technique can produce a positive effect, especially when used with children who don't want to listen or comply or people who need help changing certain behaviors.

What are the signs of Reverse Psychology?

You can probably recall at least one time when it seemed like someone was trying to get you to do something but was being indirect about it. How did that make you feel?

If it seemed like you were being manipulated to the point that it served the other person's interests more than your own, it's helpful to be aware of some of the signs of reverse psychology.

Here are a few questions to consider the next time you find yourself in a potentially manipulative situation:

- Does the person seem more relaxed and open than usual? Is this possibly an attempt to get you to trust them?
- Are they being overly negative about something to get a strong reaction out of you?

- Are they suddenly pressing for you to do something that they are normally against?
- Has their request become so persistent that you feel compelled to do the exact opposite of what you're being asked to do?
- When weighing how to respond, does one outcome benefit the other person more than yourself?

Examples of Reverse Psychology

Reverse psychology can show up in many ways and in many areas of life. Here are some examples:

Marketing

Reverse psychology is often used as a marketing tactic.

A common example is an extravagant sales pitch that sells many enticing components that you would be compelled to purchase if only you could afford it.

Instead, you end up buying something less significant from the salesperson, which, if they were using reverse psychology, is exactly what they wanted you to do.

If you're on a budget and weren't intending to make any additional purchases this month, then this form of reverse psychology has placed an unwanted strain on your finances.

Parenting

If a child refuses to get dressed for school in the morning, you could tell them that they don't have to. You could casually point out that they'll be the only kid in class wearing their pajamas.

This approach could help persuade the child to change out of their pajamas and into regular clothes since they might realize that they don't want to be singled out at school.

As a result, the child has been empowered to get dressed for school and may be more likely to continue to do so moving forward.

Relationships

Using reverse psychology in a relationship can be dangerous and should be approached with caution.

For example, your partner insists they don't want a birthday gift, but in reality, they do. To surprise your partner, you buy them a gift anyway, which, as it turns out, is actually what they really wanted you to do.

However, if your partner continues to tell you that they don't want a gift on every single birthday, then you might eventually stop buying gifts, which would disappoint your partner since they actually wanted you to get them something.

The misunderstanding that could ensue could lead to anger and resentment, making birthdays a point of contention rather than a cause for celebration.

Another example: Say your partner says they'll go grocery shopping, when in fact, they don't have time and don't really want to, which sends you to the store instead.

While this can work on occasion, if you're the one who's always going to the store, you might start to feel taken advantage of — especially if this leads to an imbalance in the distribution of household responsibilities.

How to use Reverse Psychology?

When a person is resistant by nature, whether they're a young child or an older adult, it can be helpful to employ some reverse psychology.

To use reverse psychology on a person who is especially resistant, you can try a strategy known as "reinforcing autonomy."

Reinforcing autonomy is a key aspect of a counseling technique called motivational interviewing (MI), which is often used to help treat addiction.

Research from 2012 suggests that motivational interviewing can help people work through any resistance or uncertainty around behaviors that may have a negative effect on their well-being.

Motivational interviewing is a conversational approach to persuasion. The interviewer asks strategic questions to steer the person toward positive solutions. The technique reinforces autonomy since the interviewee feels they have personal agency over their response.

To try motivational interviewing in the context of reverse psychology, you would make a suggestion or ask a question that goes against how you would like the person to answer or what you would like them to do.

For example, you're worried about the health of a loved one who is resistant to making changes to their diet and getting regular exercise.

Instead of saying "I really think you should start taking care of yourself," you could try, "Only you know what's best for you. If you could make changes to your lifestyle that would help you feel better and have more energy, what might those be?"

The result is that you've empowered your loved one to make their own choices. You've got them thinking about what they think might be good for them and have reinforced their autonomy.

In this instance, a motivational interviewing approach to reverse psychology is more helpful than simply telling a person they should just eat whatever they want and that they don't need to exercise.

When is Reverse Psychology harmful?

While reverse psychology is effective, it can sometimes cause harm, especially among those with low self-esteem and young children who may be more affected by influence.

Some children might start to pick up on the manipulation tactics of reverse psychology used by adults and use them to exploit or take advantage of other children.

In addition, many people are sensitive to passive-aggressive behavior and indirect communication and might feel like they're being controlled.

When reverse psychology becomes underhanded, reactance could lead to distrust. Relationships could become damaged if it becomes clear that the influencing person was working in their own interests only.

There are some cases, however, when a person might feel pressured to use reverse psychology, particularly when it could benefit another person.

For example, you are the parent of a college student who is contemplating dropping out. You might tell them they should just drop out and could probably find a job working minimum wage, move back home, and pay a portion of rent. Your child might decide on their own to just stay in school to avoid moving back home.

While this can be an appropriate scenario for some young people, it may not be the best outcome for others. Of course, there's also a chance that your attempt could backfire and your child drops out anyway. As an alternative approach, motivational interviewing might be more effective in this instance. Try to express genuine curiosity and ask your child what they would like to do with their time instead of going to school.

CHAPTER 10

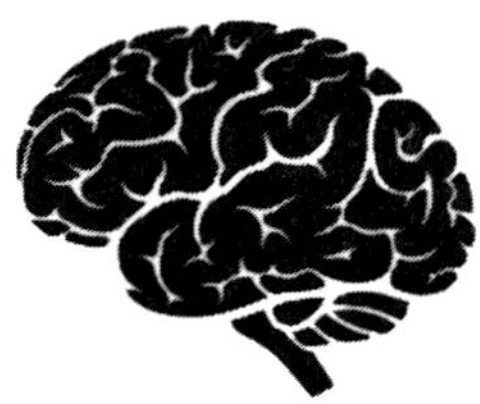

LOVE AND RELATIONSHIPS

How to manipulate a man and get him to do what you want?

Learning how to manipulate men and that special man in your life can seem uncomfortable, but if you understand how simple it is, you'll see how effortless it can be! Women have been stuck with the 'weaker gender' tag since forever. But that view is heading for a complete makeover these days because women now know how to manipulate men and get things their way!

1. Bore him to submission

Keep on talking and don't stop. Go all out when you try and explain yourself when you want to manipulate men. This works very well, especially at times when you've picked up something really expensive, and your man doesn't approve of it.

2. "I did it for you!"

Any and every time you do something wrong, just let him know that the sole purpose of doing that was to please him. How were you to know that he wouldn't appreciate the surprise holiday you booked for the both of you? How were you to know he wouldn't like your new handbag or that luxurious perfume?

3. Make him prove you wrong

Men hate being told that there's something that they can't do. And they absolutely love to prove you wrong. So don't worry about how to manipulate men here. Just tell him that he may be right, because now that you think of it.

4. "You are my saviour"

Okay, you don't have to repeat the exact words, but let's face it, men have epic egos. It's in-built, so rather than complain about it, use flattery to your advantage while manipulating men.

5. "Fine! I'll do it on my own!"

Emotional blackmail. Guys can't stand it, but they also can't do anything about it. So the next time he says he won't help you with something, don't fly off into a fit of fuming rage.

Just manipulate his mind and say, "Fine, I'll go alone, because none of my other friends are free. If they were free,

I wouldn't have asked you anyways. It may be a little late in the evening, but then, that's okay. It's not like the city is not safe for girls to travel alone."

6. Get his mom on your side

When the two most important women in his life are in it together, there is little that a guy can offer in terms of resistance. Most guys, even the ones who are not mamma's boys, still think twice before messing with their mum. So go ahead, be real nice to the in-laws.

7. Foodie manipulation

If there is something you really really want him to do, but you know he'll refuse straight away, cook him a nice fancy dinner, light a few candles. It will be one tough thing for him to say no, and he won't. Not unless his life depends on it!

8. Blame it on biology!

One of the best things about being a woman is that you can yell at him, act all pricey, irritated, and peevish, and blame it all on him. Guys can't contradict it, because they don't understand it.

9. Shed a tear

It is a girl's best friend in all messy situations and manipulative situations. He's yelling at you at the top of his voice. And you know, this time it really is your fault. But you also know that saying sorry won't shut him up. So bring out a tear or two, and most guys will stop. Most guys don't really know what to do with a crying woman. And their first priority in such a case is to make her stop. More so, if she's crying because of something that they've said. Even if they still think they are right, they will shut up. And they will be careful the next time they broach the topic.

10. Seduce him!

Why waste time talking about all the stupid things that you always talk about. Just tell him you want him, and you want him right now!

And before you know it, you would know how to manipulate men to do your whims and fancies. At the end of the day, always remember that people manipulate each other, but to have the best effect while manipulating men, use these tried and tested ways to get things your way!

How to manipulate women with low self-esteem into liking you?

Women always fall for the bad guy. It is hard for them to resist the wrong guys. Have you ever wondered why? Because, women can be easily manipulated! Not all women, but mostly women with low self-esteem. Women prefer a lot of drama in their love life. Women wish to have a fairy tale love life, which truly never really exists. They fail to notice that, but it is not their fault, it is just the basic built up idea that we all live in.

Eye contact to manipulate women into liking you

If you are trying to manipulate women with low self-esteem into liking you, then the best rule will be to hold intense eye contact with her. Make it look natural and let her understand that you are into her. Don't try it hard and end up looking creepy. Make sure it sends her the right message.

Show a little interest in her

Men might seem desperate especially when they are with pretty women. So, if you tend to show no interest in her it is going to drive her nuts. Make sure she notices you but you try and neglect her presence. This might make her curious and might make her wonder why isn't he interested in me? This is one of the ways that you can manipulate women with low self-esteem.

Get her to notice you

When trying to manipulate a low self-esteem women into liking you, make her come to you. Never give women the chance to choose and reject. It is time you take things into your hands. Try to get her to notice you by disagreeing with her. Let her know her choices were wrong or she has made a mistake. This way she will not only notice you but will try to impress you and prove to you that she was right.

Jealousy can manipulate women with low self-esteem

Having met the girl of your dreams and if you are trying to trick her into being your girlfriend, then you need to make her jealous. Jealousy can make any girl fall in love. The fear of losing someone will make her hold your complete attention. So, whenever your girlfriend is around, be flirtatious with other girls to make her jealous. This is one of the ways you can manipulate women with low self-esteem into liking you.

Try to confuse her

If you want to get the girl you like to be your girlfriend, always send her mixed signals. Never be clear with your way of expressing your feelings for her. Make her feel loved, at the same time, make it look very casual. She should feel confused with what is actually happening with you. She must try to figure out the exact feelings you have for her. Who doesn't want to feel loved? So does your girl, she will want to know whether she is being loved or was it your friendly nature. This is one of the ways to manipulate your woman with low self-esteem into liking you.

Be a little mysterious

To get women curious you need to look a little mysterious. Be a little secretive never let her know anything about you. Just give a few hints but never reveal anything completely. Use her curiosity to develop more interest in you. By being mysterious you force her to think about you, which develops an interest in you. So, always seem a little mysterious when she is around. So, this is one of the ways that you can easily manipulate your women into liking you.

Make her feel left out to manipulate women

When trying to manipulate your girl into liking you, you need to make her feel left out. Be nice to everybody around her, but never bother to talk with her. This way you will make her feel left out. This will make her think that there is something wrong with her that you dislike, so she might try to get your attention. When you give her your attention she might welcome it with a lot of joy.

Be commanding when you try to manipulate women

When trying to manipulate women with low self-esteem, be dominating. Let your girlfriend know that you have a happy single life and that you rejoice it, so she might know what to do and what not to do. The earlier you set the control the happiest you can be. Never always give her a chance to control, rather take things in your hand and set boundaries.

Get her sympathy vote

When you want to manipulate your low self-esteem women into liking you then you need to get her sympathy. Women show compassion and when used it at the right time you get their complete attention and care. Tell her a sad story that has ever happened to you. Put in a little drama and try to get her aid. Let her know that you have some sorrows and how you have overcome those struggles. By doing this you get to have a permanent place in her heart.

Admit that you are in love with her

Everyone loves to be told that they are in love. So, tell your women that you are in love with her. Reveal the little secret to your girlfriend but don't expect her to give you any results right away. Tell her that she is loved so deeply and that she has always been the one for him. Women believe in head over heels love and they appreciate it when there is a lot of drama in it. This is one of the ways that you can manipulate your women who have low self-esteem into liking you.

Be confident when trying to manipulate women

Women love men who are confident, it is a major factor that attracts them. To make yourself lovable you need to be a confident person who is worth being around with. Live your life in a way that she feels the need to be with you. Make her feel that being with you might make her life even more amazing. If you want to manipulate your low self-esteem women into liking you then you need to be a confident person.

Play the hardball

When you want to manipulate your girl into liking you, then you need to play the hardball game. Make her feel that you are undesirable and never really easy to impress. Turn her down when she asks for a drive home, to fix her car or even when she invites for coffee. By rejecting her favors or requests you make her feel that you are someone very special and that she must try hard to get you. This is one of the ways to trick your women with low self-esteem.

Make her feel that you are amazing

If you want to make the girl of your dreams as your girlfriend, then all you need to do is make her believe that you are amazing. Show her how amazing her life will be when she is with you. Make her feel that her life with you is way better than her fantasy. If you make her believe, life with you can be adventurous and fascinating, women with low self-esteem tend to fall in love with you. This is one of the ways to manipulate your women with low self-esteem.

Make physical contact with her

When you have a love interest in your low self-esteem women to manipulate her into liking you, you need to make your move. She will never understand your interest unless you make physical contact with her. Touch her, caress her make it look very natural and casual. Give her subtle hints that you have feelings for her. Women with low self-esteem can be easily manipulated into liking you with this simple trick.

Work on her emotions to manipulate women

To manipulate a woman with low self-esteem you need to understand her emotions better. You need to observe the way she reacts to different situations. Know how to deal with her, know what will make her happy or what will make her sad. Throw in a happy memory of hers and make her happy and instantly recall a sad memory and make her sad. This way you can easily learn to control her by manipulating her, using her emotions.

Be a little dramatic

Women tend to fall for the guys who make grand gestures to show their love. So, if you want to manipulate her into liking you, you need to show her that you love her with a lot of drama. Take her by surprise; make it a big deal when it comes to expressing your interest. It will help you to win her heart easily and she will be letting you take a complete control of her life. This is one of the ways you can manipulate your woman with low self-esteem.

Make her listen to you

To make your woman listen to you, all you need is to express your emotions; happy ones, angry ones or even sad ones. Let her comfort you, the sadder you feel, the more comfort you are going to get from her. The happier you express your own self; the happier it gets for her. When in rage, she might want to lift your mood and hopefully, you will end up having a good time with her. Never be the one who always listens to her stories, make her listen to yours once in a while. This is one of the ways to manipulate women with low self-esteem into liking you.

Be online but never respond immediately

To drive women crazy, you need to send a text message or even chat over social media accounts like Facebook, Hangouts and never respond immediately. Leave her expecting for messages from you. You need to have a great conversation with her and then follow this technique. If you leave her without any reply immediately after having started the conversation it might not be effective. So, first build an interesting conversation and then don't respond her immediately. Be online but give her a delayed response, it will drive her nuts. This is one of the most common ways in trend to manipulate women with low self-esteem.

Don't see her regularly

If you want your women to long for you, you should never be available for her. Make it a point never to meet her or see her on a regular basis. Skip a day or two in the middle so she develops the curiosity to see you and she will be forced to think about why you have not showed up. This is one of the ways to manipulate women with low self-esteem.

Tell her she is different

Women love to feel special and unique but men fail to do that. To manipulate a low self-esteem women tell her that she is unique from all the women you have met so far. Tell her that she is the women you have always hoped for falling in love with. Make sure she understands that you believe that she is someone special from all the other women you have met so far. By doing this you can easily manipulate your women into liking you.

Stand up for her

When trying to manipulate women with low self-esteem, stand up for her. Whenever she is criticized or being judged by others, protect her, never let others speak ill of her. This way you will easily impress your woman with low self-esteem as she might be having her own insecurities. By standing up for her you reassure her that you can keep her in safe space.

Mirror her actions

If you want your low self-esteem woman into liking you, mirror her actions. Copy her actions, by doing this you impress her and also you can easily trick her into liking you. By pacing her you send her a secret message that you are into her. Mirror her body language, her emotions, this will help you to make her feel special and she will start to like you. So, if you are thinking about ways to manipulate low self-esteem women into liking you, this is one of the easiest ways.

Disappear for a few days

After getting to know your girl, if you want her to miss you terribly then you need to disappear from her for a few days. Make it a point not to send her a message or call her when you have disappeared. Tell your friends not to give away any information about you. This way she will try to reach you and start looking for you and will miss you when you are not around. This is one of the ways to manipulate your woman into liking you.

Be charming

Everyone loves to be with people who are charming and fun loving. Be the kind of person when you are around your low self-esteem woman. Always be approachable and have a big fat smile on your face to manipulate her into thinking you are adorable. Love yourself, any women will fall in love with you, if you really love who you are. This is one of the ways to manipulate women into liking you.

So, make sure that you have thought about both the pros and cons before you actually execute the ways for manipulating your woman into liking you.

CHAPTER 11

THE DARK FACTOR OF PERSONALITY

The Dark (or D) Factor of Personality is a basic psychological personality trait and thus relatively consistent across situations and stable across time. Elevated levels in D predispose individuals towards a broad range of socially and ethically aversive thoughts and behaviors, such as aggression, bullying, cheating, crime, stealing, vandalism, violence, and many others.

D is defined as the tendency to "maximize one's individual utility—disregarding, accepting, or malevolently provoking disutility for others —, accompanied by beliefs that serve as justifications." Utility refers to the extent to which individuals achieve their goals, and disutility is the extent to which goal-achievement is hindered. Goals can be more or less tangible (e.g. money, status, or power vs. excitement, joy, or pleasure). Whereas aiming to achieve one's goals is an aspect of normal psychological functioning, individuals with elevated levels in D will be inclined to harm other individuals or groups in pursuing their goals, i.e., they will cause disutility on others. For example, stealing something causes financial disutility, bullying someone causes psychological disutility, and hurting someone causes physiological disutility. Individuals high in D might even experience own utility (such as excitement) from disutility inflicted on others (such as pain).

In order to maintain a positive (moral) self-image despite engaging in aversive or malevolent behavior towards others, high-D individuals hold beliefs that they deem suited to justify their behavior. Such beliefs include, for instance, considering oneself (or one's group) as superior and entitled, endorsing ideologies favoring dominance of individuals or groups, viewing the world as a dangerous place and competitive jungle, believing that others are stupid or somehow losers and, in turn, deserve to be exploited, and many more. These beliefs allow individuals high in D to act in ways that harm others without feelings of guilt or remorse, and thereby contribute to the maintenance of malevolent behavior.

Relation to other aversive traits

According to the D theory, D reflects the basic disposition underlying any aversive trait (such as Machiavellianism, narcissism, or psychopathy), which are regarded as specific expressions ("flavored manifestations") of D. As a consequence, D reflects what all aversive traits have in common, i.e., the aversive part of any trait. This implies that any aversive trait comprises the features of D, but also potentially other components that are largely unrelated to D and are thus not aversive as such. For example, psychopathy is aversive because it reflects D to some extent, but it additionally comprises features related to disinhibition or impulsivity, which – in isolation - do not systematically lead to aversive behavior. However, combined with D (determining whether aversive behavior occurs), impulsivity co-determines how and under which conditions such behavior is displayed.

Measurement

D is usually measured relying on self-reports. Because D is assumed to be responsible for the occurrence of aversive behavior, it will be reflected in all indicators used to assess aversive traits, albeit to varying degrees. However, although the indicators of any particular aversive trait will also reflect D, measuring D itself requires the inclusion of a sufficiently large number of diverse indicators in order to capture the full theoretical breadth that D represents. Thus, item sets that allow for a reliable and valid assessment of D have been compiled and are available in many languages, and also as an online self-assessment

CHAPTER 12

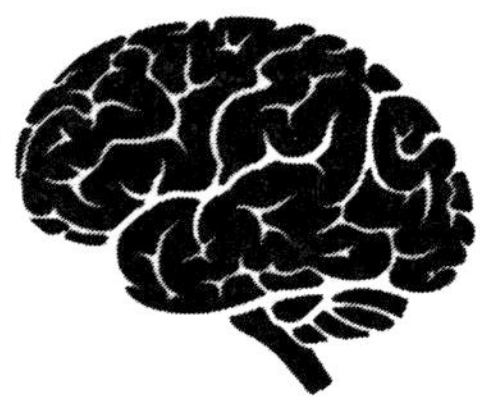

HOW TO PROTECT YOURSELF FROM EMOTIONAL MANIPULATION?

Emotional manipulation happens when someone seeks to gain power or control by employing certain tactics. Usually, it involves gaslighting, passive aggression, and emotional abuse such as name-calling. A 2013 study found that emotional abuse can cause just as much harm as physical abuse, leading to depression and poor self-image. Unfortunately, emotional abuse occurs often in relationships, with 47% of women and almost 47% of men experiencing it at some point.

Warning Signs that Reveal Emotional Manipulation

1. Intellectual Bullying reveals Emotional Manipulation

Some emotional manipulators will attempt to gain power over you through intellectual bullying. Basically, this just means they bombard you with facts and knowledge to confuse or overwhelm you. When you're in a vulnerable state, it makes you much easier to control. Many narcissists use this tactic, and may even quiz you about certain topics. They're trying to gauge how much you know to see how you measure up against them.

2. Emotional Invalidation

Emotional manipulation can also take the form of invalidation, where the person tries to downplay your feelings or experiences. For example, if you're explaining how you fell at work and they immediately shift the focus on themselves, they're trying to manipulate you. It might seem innocent at first, but their intentions will become clear eventually.

People who compare your issues with theirs want to garner sympathy but can't seem to show it. It's best to steer clear of people who invalidate your problems, especially if they claim to care about your well-being. If they did, they would show it through their actions.

3. Gaslighting and Playing the Victim

If a person gaslights you, it's a clear sign they're engaging in emotional manipulation. Gaslighting involves making the victim question their own sanity by twisting stories or creating false narratives. Of course, they want you to feel crazy in order to maintain control. They don't want to take accountability for any problems in the relationship, blaming you for anything that goes wrong.

If you bring up a concern, they will immediately downplay your feelings or even deny their wrongdoing. They want you to feel responsible for any mistakes to lower your self-esteem even further. You know in your gut when something feels off in a relationship, so please don't fall for this manipulation technique.

4. Shaming can be a Sign of Emotional Manipulation

Emotional manipulators want you to feel inferior, guilty and shameful so they have power over your emotions. When they know they can get a rise out of you, it becomes an addiction. They will always crave more because they enjoy seeing you upset.

Like any energy vampire, they thrive off negative emotional reactions and people with compassion. Emotional manipulators usually target empathetic victims since they tend to see the positives in others. That way, they're blindsided when the manipulation begins since they never saw it coming.

The manipulator may shame you by saying you're ungrateful for everything they've done for you. They want you to feel obligated to them in some way, but in reality, you only owe yourself the freedom to leave this toxic relationship.

5. Lying

While a white lie here and there doesn't always point to emotional manipulation, it's a red flag when it happens repeatedly. The person may lie to hide something they feel ashamed about, such as cheating. Or if they're a compulsive liar, they've learned to make up stories out of habit, either to embellish or deny facts. Either way, lying about important things in relationships can create a rift between people over time.

Trust forms the foundation in a healthy relationship, and once the lies accumulate, it begins to crack. Sure, you can repair things after one or two lies, but at some point, the trust disappears completely. Just remember, if someone truly loves and cares about you, they'll tell you the truth no matter how much it hurts. They'd rather come clean than walk around with a heart full of secrets.

6. Using Ultimatums

Another common form of emotional manipulation involves giving someone ultimatums. The manipulator does this to find your weaknesses so they can get what they want. For instance, your partner might say they will break up with you if you go out for girl's night. Not only does this point to a controlling partner, it also shows they have deep-seated insecurities. Or, perhaps they might ask for financial help, saying that "If you love me, you'll do this for me."

Of course, someone who uses ultimatums doesn't have your best interests at heart.

7. Giving Silent Treatment

A common passive aggressive behavior, the silent treatment is used to gain control in a relationship. This form of emotional manipulation may occur after an argument or disagreement, especially if the person felt unheard. They want to shift all the attention onto themselves and gain sympathy by refusing to communicate with you.

The manipulator figures that, after a while, you will come crawling back to them and apologize for your behavior. They want you to feel responsible, even if the argument was their fault. Eventually, you might feel worried about them and decide to break the silence. This is what they had planned all along, of course, so that you'd forget about the underlying issues and admit your mistake.

If you're in a relationship with someone who employs the silent treatment often, let them know it bothers you. Relationships are a two-way street and require active communication from both people.

Ways to Protect Yourself from Emotional Manipulation

1. Don't fall into their trap.

People who take pleasure in toying with others' emotions will use any sort of tactics, such as confusion, blame, and interrogation, in order to really get under your skin. If you have to deal with these types of people often, like in your workplace, just ignore them or surprise them by saying something nice instead of meeting them with a combative attitude. Emotional manipulators thrive off getting a rise out of you, so make sure you don't give them what they want – after several failed attempts, they may begin to leave you alone.

2. Start writing down what they say during conversations.

While this might seem a little overboard, emotional manipulators have a habit of making you look like the bad guy, and twisting their words to fit any agenda. You might actually start to believe sometimes that you have done something wrong when in reality, you have fallen victim to their terrible scheme. To make sure you can actually show them what they said in prior conversations, jot down any details you think they might conveniently change later in order to justify their behavior. They may also try to convince you they never said a certain thing, but you can actually prove they did with the notes you take.

Get smart about protecting yourself from their wrath, and they may soon get discouraged from using you as their emotional toy.

3. Steer clear whenever possible.

Of course, avoiding emotional manipulators and instigators will totally eliminate your chances of getting taken advantage of by them. To do this, try your best to read people's energy when you first meet them. If you don't get a good vibe from them, simply trust your gut and make a pact to steer clear of them when you can. Working in the same place as an emotional manipulator can be a bit trickier, but just aim to limit your interactions with the person as much as possible. You will save yourself a lot of energy and sanity by doing so.

4. Call them out on their behavior.

These people have probably bossed around others for so long and have never been confronted for it. Stand up for yourself and let them know that they make you feel uncomfortable and taken advantage of. Even if they deny their behavior or try to turn it back around on you, at least you can rest easy knowing you actually defended yourself and stood up for the truth. Maybe they will begin to change their tune if you struck a nerve with them; after all, once they scare everyone away, they will have no one to manipulate anymore, anyway.

5. Avoid emotional attachment with them.

Easier said than done, especially if they don't show their true colors immediately. Pay attention to the first sign of them completely steamrolling your emotions, slowly back away from the relationship, and make sure to let them know your boundaries. Emotional manipulators constantly scan the horizon for their next victim, but it's much easier to break away if you haven't invested too much in the relationship, to begin with. If you must talk to them, maintain a cordial, civil relationship, but don't let it go any further than that if you value your emotional well-being.

6. Meditate often.

In order to keep your vibration high, you need to silence the mind, breathe deeply, and get in touch with the higher realms to adequately handle yourself on Earth. It will help you deal with emotional manipulators much better because you will have inner peace no matter how much chaos unfolds around you. Loving-kindness meditation, specifically, will allow you to cultivate compassion for this person and maybe open your eyes to what they have been through in their life. Meet hostility with love and understanding, and you just might witness them to transform into a new person after a while.

7. Inspire them.

It's important to "be the change", and in this instance, it will inadvertently protect you because they won't emit such negative vibes after they're inspired by your own non-manipulative, positive actions. Bring up the benefits of meditation, taking responsibility for their own life, following their true passions, volunteering, eating a clean diet, and exercising. Use all the knowledge you have gained about becoming your best self in order to help them become their best selves, too.

8. Tell them "you're right."

As hard as this might be for the ego, your soul will give you a round of applause and possibly a standing ovation, too. Emotional manipulators feed on drama, so agreeing with them will leave them speechless and quickly put out the flames of their delusions. Just for the sake of keeping your peace of mind, simply let them win the argument. You know deep down that their behavior and accusations were wrong, but they will have to deal with that karma later anyway.

9. Let go of harmful relationships.

If you notice this type of behavior in your boyfriend, girlfriend, or spouse, you should leave that relationship behind in favor of your own well-being. You can't force a person to change, no matter how many times you have brought up their volatile behavior. You deserve someone who will nurture and balance your emotions, not someone who wants to use you for their own personal enjoyment.

10. Develop a strong mentality.

Don't ever let their insults or outbursts get inside your head; laugh at them or just entertain their thoughts without agreeing with them. If you know what kind of person you are and have a strong sense of self-worth, nothing they say will ever bring you down.

11. Give yourself positive self-talk throughout the day.

An emotional manipulator can completely tarnish your otherwise peppy mood, so make sure you restore yourself with uplifting affirmations and messages during the day. They thrive on seeing your mood go down the drain, so when they see you unaffected by their brash remarks, they won't have a reason to torment you any longer.

Unfortunately, emotional manipulation occurs quite often in schools, workplaces, and relationships. Many of us have probably manipulated people without even realizing it as well, because no one is perfect. However, when someone intentionally deceives others with the goal of getting something from them, it becomes a form of abuse. In daily life, it's important to shield yourself from negative people and walk away from anyone who doesn't have your best interests at heart.

Emotional manipulators usually reveal themselves much like narcissists do, by lying, gaslighting, invalidating your feelings, or shaming you. Don't fall for these tactics, as they can only derive power by steamrolling over others.

CHAPTER 13

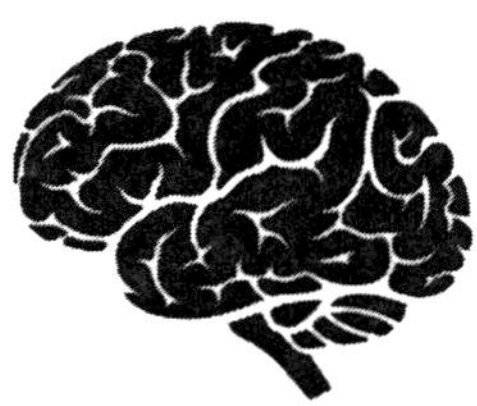

WHAT IS PERSUASION?

Persuasion is a process in which one person tries to influence another person or group of people to change their beliefs or behaviors. It is distinct from coercion, in that the people receiving the message have a choice about whether to act on it.

Persuasion can be a powerful force that affects the decisions and actions that people take. Persuasive messages are symbolic (using words, images, and sounds) and may be transmitted verbally or non-verbally, via media or face-to-face communication. Persuasion may be overt or subtle. Understanding how it works can help you become more aware of how you are influenced by persuasive messages.

6 Principles of Persuasion

Psychologists recognize six characteristics of persuasion, originally identified by Robert Cialdini in 1984. These principles describe what makes persuasive messages influential and successful. Some persuasive efforts may use several of these tactics simultaneously.

Reciprocity

As humans, we tend to repay others when they have done something for us. You might easily persuade a friend to do a favor for you if you have already done one for them. In a business context, reciprocity could mean being willing to provide your email address in order to receive a discount on your purchase.

Scarcity

You might be persuaded to change your behavior if you are convinced that you will lose access to something, or that there isn't enough of it to go around. You can see this principle in action when an airline alerts you that there are only a few seats left on a flight you're considering, or a retailer advertises a limited-time sale.

Authority

If you believe that a person has expert knowledge, you may be more likely to be persuaded by their message. An advertiser or political candidate might use an authority figure, such as a physician, historian, or scientist, to support their argument.

Consistency or Commitment

People have a tendency to continue their previous behavior or stick with a decision they have made. In an interview, Cialdini gave a example of this involving a restaurant that struggled with no-shows.

When a patron made a reservation, if the receptionist asked them to call if they needed to cancel (and got an affirmative reply), they were much less likely to miss their reservation. The patrons were effectively making a promise, and were committed to keeping it.

Social Proof

This is the "safety in numbers" principle. If we see that our friends or peers have made a purchase, supported a political candidate, or otherwise agreed with a persuasive message, we may be more likely to agree with it too.

Liking

If you know and like the person (or even business, political party, or government agency) trying to persuade you of something, you will be more inclined to agree with their argument. This is similar to the "social proof" principle, but is more about the quality of the relationship, where social proof is about quantity.

Signs of Persuasion

Political campaigns, mass media, social media, and advertising all use the power of persuasion to influence us. Sometimes we like to believe that we are immune to persuasion, that we can see through the sales pitch, comprehend the truth in a situation, and come to conclusions all on our own.

This might be true in some scenarios, when an attempt at persuasion is clear: You know that a salesperson's job is to sell you something, and that a campaign ad is designed to persuade you to vote for a candidate. A social media influencer's sponsored content may be clearly labeled as such.

But persuasive messages can also be subtle. Look for elements of the six principles of persuasion to identify an attempt to persuade you. This might mean phrases such as "limited availability" (scarcity), "doctors say" (authority), or "customers agree" (social proof),

Uses

Advertisements that urge viewers to buy a particular product are a form of persuasion. So are political debates, where candidates try to sway voters to their side. Persuasion is a powerful force in daily life and has a major influence on society and a whole.

Negative examples of persuasion often come to mind—as in an ad trying to get you to buy something you don't need, peer pressure that causes you to make a poor decision, or even deliberate misinformation. But persuasion can also be used in a positive way: Think of public service or health campaigns that urge people to recycle, quit smoking, or practice social distancing to help protect themselves and their community.

How to Respond to Persuasion?

Being informed about persuasion and persuasive techniques can help you recognize persuasion and respond to it. It can also help you use it to influence the behavior of others.

Evaluate Information Carefully

When you are trying to make a decision (about something big, like who to vote for, or small, like what movie to watch), gather information to help you make a wise choice. But be thoughtful and even skeptical about that information. Who is providing it, and what is their motivation? Do they stand to gain in some way from your choice? Be sure you trust your sources.

How to Resist Persuasion?

Being aware of persuasive techniques and of the trustworthiness of information used to make choices can help you resist persuasion. It's also important to be willing to change your mind. Feeling burdened by sunk costs—or the perception that you've already invested too much in a decision to be able to back out—could lead you to be persuaded to go against your better judgment.

People who are impulsive may be more susceptible to persuasion than others. Similarly, people who lack self-control also tend to be susceptible to persuasion. So taking steps to improve your self-control can help you resist persuasion.

How to use Persuasion?

You can use your knowledge of persuasion to convince others to align with your point of view. For example, if you want your partner to visit a new restaurant with you, you could remind them that a friend whose opinion they trust recommended the place (liking), that it has dozens of positive reviews from other diners (social proof), or that they chose the restaurant last time (reciprocity).

Your knowledge and understanding of your audience (in this case, your partner) can help you decide which persuasive techniques will be most effective. For instance, maybe your partner doesn't care about what other diners think, but they do hate to miss out on something unusual. In that case, you might try a scarcity tactic: "This specialty dish is only available on Sundays, and only to the first ten diners."

Research shows that projecting confidence via your tone of voice makes you more persuasive. Even if you don't feel confident in your argument, sounding as if you do helps you succeed.

CHAPTER 14

MODES OF PERSUASION

Over two thousand years ago, a famous Greek teacher, Aristotle, taught his students that there were three basic ways of convincing your audience of something—or at least getting your audience to listen to what you have to say. We still use these concepts today. You will often hear ethos, pathos, and logos referred to as the three modes of persuasion.

These modes of persuasion will probably come quite naturally to you, but having a strong awareness of how to be most convincing to your audience will help you as you write argumentative essays.

Ethos

Ethos is a way of convincing your audience of your credibility as a writer. Some credibility can be, in a way, built-in. Level of education in relation to the topic may provide some built-in ethos. For example, if a Psychology professor were writing an essay about the psychology of eating disorders, she or he would have strong, built-in ethos. But, if that same professor were to try to write a paper on quantum physics, her or his educational background would provide no built-in ethos.

You need not worry if you have no built-in ethos or credibility. There is also the kind of ethos or credibility you work to establish as you write. By using appeals to emotion and logic responsibly, you can build your ethos. You can also build your ethos by using credible sources. When you use expert research and opinion in your writing, you get to use the expert ethos to build your own.

Pathos

Most simply, pathos is the appeal to our human emotions. We're more often moved by our emotions than by logic or common sense, so pathos is a powerful mode of persuasion. As a writer, your job is to make the audience feel connected with your topic. This is where pathos can help. Think about the broad spectrum of human emotions: sadness, humor, pity, sympathy, anger, outrage; these are all things that motivate us. Pathos provides writers with a tool to get the audience emotionally invested in the message.

Pathos is a powerful means of persuasion. But you should be very careful with pathos. Pathos is generally the least respected of the three ethical appeals in the academic community. In many fields of study, emotion is something that should be left out completely. Most of the time, the best advice is to be careful with pathos and use it wisely. Misusing pathos can negatively affect your ethos or credibility.

Logos

Logos is the appeal to our logical side. Logos is about the facts we present in our writing and the logical manner in which we present our ideas. Having strong logos is one important way that we can build our ethos within an essay. For example, if you're writing a research paper on the **Plague in Medieval Times**, you'll want to gather a good deal of research and then incorporate that research in an organized and effective manner. You should also make sure that your points or arguments are logical in nature, and you should avoid faulty logic.

Ethos, pathos, and logos are all interconnected. When you write an argument, you'll want to think about how these modes of persuasion work together to make for a strong argument overall.

Some examples of Persuasion

In your day-to-day life, you may come across a variety of situations where you persuade others or others persuade you. Given below are some common examples:

- Written, visual and media advertisements are persuasive methods used by marketing professionals to influence a customer's purchase decision.

- Large-scale campaigns for social causes like cancer awareness, sustainability and vaccination drives involve organised efforts to persuade diverse audiences. The persuaders may use one or more formats like posters, videos, public demonstrations, television advertisements and podcasts to subtly promote ideas and concepts that they align with.

- Speeches, articles and videos of motivational speakers are examples of their persuasion skills in action.
- Salespeople use their persuasion skills to convert potential customers into loyal patrons of their brand.
- Teachers, mentors and counsellors persuade students to engage well with their academic curriculum and make good career decisions.
- Business owners and top executives may use persuasion during business deals and negotiations to safeguard their business interests.
- Team managers use persuasion to motivate their team members to complete work on or ahead of schedule.

What skills do you require to persuade others?

Persuasion skills can be a natural talent or personality trait. You can also develop and master this skill with adequate practice and determination. These skills help you convince someone to carry out an action or consider an idea. Organizations often employ people with persuasion skills to sell products, get new clients, recruit new employees and increase productivity. A person with strong persuasion skills at their workplace can motivate and inspire colleagues to perform better and succeed at their work. Here are some important skills that can help you become a good persuader:

- Communication skills
- Emotional intelligence

- Active listening skills
- Logical reasoning ability
- Interpersonal skills
- Negotiation skills

How to improve Persuasion skills?

To be an effective persuader, you can enhance and master the skills mentioned above. This may require time and practice. Here are some ways in which you can improve your persuasion skills:

1. Develop your communication skills

Speaking with intent and confidence can help you persuade others effectively. Speak clearly to avoid confusion, and only use non-verbal gestures that the other person can understand easily. Use vocabulary that is simple and positive. Focus on building credibility, rather than intimidating listeners.

While sharing ideas, be engaging and use a tone that appeals to the listener. List the positive features of your idea and refrain from demeaning theirs. For example, if you are selling a product, talk extensively about how your product is better and sparingly about the shortcomings of the product they already own. Honouring and respecting a customer's purchasing decisions can help build trust.

2. Build emotional intelligence

When you are trying to persuade someone, evaluate their feelings and emotions before you speak. With enough practice, you can respond to situations appropriately and customize your persuasion tactics according to the specific situation you are in. While some individuals may appreciate a matter-of-fact attitude and concise arguments, this need not always be the case. Some may demand a detailed explanation and may expect you to be more empathetic.

With emotional intelligence, you can gauge a person's mood and willingness to be persuaded and tailor your arguments accordingly. For example, as a manager, you may choose a reassuring tone to communicate with a nervous employee and a firm, rational tone with someone who is engaging in conflict after receiving constructive feedback. As you build emotional intelligence, you can be confident that you do not sound intimidating or patronizing to either of them.

3. Listen actively

Active listening involves being more respectful and attentive to a listener's point of view. To improve this skill, it is important to develop patience and listen to the concerns of a person without interrupting them. Give people enough time to talk about their perspectives and allow them to share their thoughts in a comprehensive, detailed manner. This can help make them comfortable in the conversation and can help you gain their trust. Once you establish trust, it often becomes significantly easier to persuade.

4. Use logic and reason to support your arguments

You can rely on logic, rational thought and verifiable facts in your argument to compel listeners to subscribe to your idea or viewpoint. Gather comprehensive data and allow the other person enough time to examine the data, interpret it and come to conclusions. Share examples and your analysis of similar situations that have happened in the past. For example, if you want to convince your manager about shifting to a new CRM (customer-relationship management) tool, talk about its benefits in terms of financial, temporal and labour costs. Consider sharing testimonials and reviews from credible sources.

5. Improve your interpersonal skills

Interpersonal skills help to interact and maintain meaningful relationships with others. They are crucial for managers and leaders who require to constantly engage with people from various departments and with others outside the organization. To improve your interpersonal skills, you can try to be genuine, behave naturally and be charismatic. The people you interact with may notice if your behavior is unnatural or forced. This reduces your credibility and your chances of being able to persuade them.

6. Master the art of negotiation

To convince people to do something, it is important to be able to show them the benefits of engaging in the actions that you are recommending. If the benefits match their expectations, your persuasion is more likely to work. To improve negotiation skills, try to gauge an individual's expectations and assess their motivation, intent and rationale for it. You can then make genuine, visible efforts to see if you or another invested party can meet their expectations.

Consider creating a list of all that you can offer and even your limitations. Once you have identified limitations, both parties can start working on a compromise. By compromising a little yourself, you can persuade the other party to reciprocate. Instead of making huge compromises in one round, try to maintain leverage while negotiating. Be prepared for multiple rounds of negotiation until you reach an arrangement that is beneficial for all parties.

CHAPTER 15

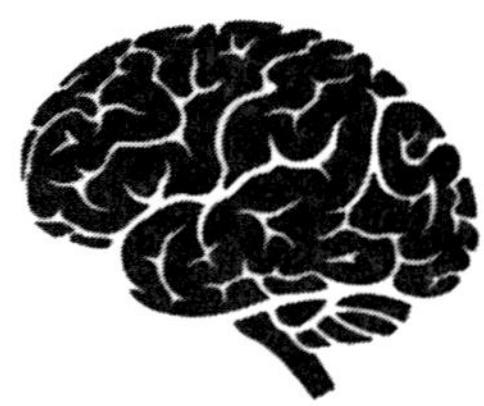

WHAT IS NEURO-LINGUISTIC PROGRAMMING (NLP)?

Neuro-linguistic programming (NLP) is the practice of understanding how people organize their thinking, feeling, language and behavior to produce the results they do. NLP provides people with a methodology to model outstanding performances achieved by geniuses and leaders in their field. NLP is also used for personal development and for success in business

A key element of NLP is that we form our unique internal mental maps of the world as a product of the way we filter and perceive information absorbed through our five senses from the world around us

Neuro

Each individual has established their own unique mental filtering system for processing the millions of bits of data being absorbed through the senses. Our first mental map of the world is constituted of internal images, sounds, tactile awareness, internal sensations, tastes and smells that form as result of the neurological filtering process. The first mental map is called **'First Access'** in NLP.

Linguistic

We then assign personal meaning to the information being received from the world outside. We form our second mental map by assigning language to the internal images, sounds and feelings, tastes and smells, thus forming everyday conscious awareness. The second mental map is called the **'Linguistic Map'** (sometimes known as Linguistic Representation)

Programming

The behavioural response that occurs as a result of neurological filtering processes and the subsequent linguistic map.

NLP Origins

Neuro Linguistic Programming began in the early 1970s when an Associate Professor from the University of California, Santa Cruz, John Grinder, teamed up with an undergraduate Richard Bandler. Both men had a fascination with human excellence which charted a path for them to model behavioral patterns of selected geniuses.

Modelling is the core activity in NLP, and is the process of extricating and replicating the language structure and behavioural patterns of an individual who is excellent at a given activity.

Grinder and Bandler began their NLP quest by modelling three people, Fritz Perls, Virginia Satir and Milton Erickson. These geniuses were outstanding as professional agents of change, working in the domain of therapy. All three geniuses, Perls, Satir and Erickson performed their magic from a perspective of unconscious excellence. The geniuses did not present Grinder and Bandler with a conscious description of their behavior. The modellers (Grinder and Bandler) unconsciously absorbed the patterning inherent in the geniuses and then provided a description.

With little direct knowledge of each of the geniuses speciality and little knowledge of the field of psychotherapy on the whole, Grinder and Bandler over a two year period set out with enthusiasm bordering on fervour, to explicate selected portions of the geniuses' behavior. They coded the results of their work in language-based models using the patterns of transformational grammar as the descriptive vocabulary. Through NLP Modelling, Grinder and Bandler made explicit the tacit skills of the geniuses and NLP was born.

The company that Grinder and Bandler were keeping in these heady days of the 1970s was a melting pot of enquiring minds seeking investigation into human behaviour. John Grinder was an associate professor at the University of California, Santa Cruz and Richard Bandler a fourth year undergraduate student. The world renowned anthropologist, Gregory Bateson had joined the faculty at Kresge College, and such was Bateson's interest in Grinder and Bandler's collaboration he introduced Grinder and Bandler to Milton Erickson. Bateson provided support, feedback and his enthusiasm is in part captured in his introduction to the book **Structure of Magic** where he states "John Grinder and Richard Bandler have done something similar to what my colleagues and I attempted fifteen years ago."

In 1975, Grinder and Bandler presented the first two NLP models to the world in the volumes **"Structure of Magic I and II."** The volumes published by the respected publishing house "Science and Behaviour Books inc" put NLP on the map and interest in the new field of NLP spread quickly. People in fields related to communication, behavior and change sought to learn how they too could get amazing results when doing change work. Grinder and Bandler willingly offered training courses in the application of their models. The training courses Bandler and Grinder conducted - proved that the NLP models were transferable to others, meaning the learners could use the NLP models successfully in their own work.

NLP Modelling

NLP modelling is the art of making explicit the set of differences present in someone who is excellent at a given activity as compared with someone who is mediocre at the same activity. NLP modelling is by far the highest skill level in NLP. NLP modelling can be used to capture patterns of excellence present in anyone in any context.

Many companies in the NLP community put little or no emphasis on modelling. Michael Carroll attended an NLP course back in 1995 and was disappointed that the trainer openly admitted he 'didn't know much about modelling'. When Michael set up the NLP Academy he ensured modelling would be an integral part of the NLP Academy philosophy. Modelling is a major feature of our Master Practitioner Course. Modelling is also featured in the NLPedia Master Practitioner Study Set.

Through the years John Grinder, has continued to develop his skills as a modeller. He stands head and shoulders above the rest of the field as a person who can capture the patterns of excellence inherent in any outstanding individual. John Grinder, with his partner Carmen Bostic St Clair, offer modelling trainings with the NLP Academy.

NLP Training

When the NLP developers began to share their knowledge, NLP Certification became available with other trainers. Thirty years after the NLP inception, modern day NLP training comes in all shapes and sizes, some excellent, some good, a lot of average and some decidedly poor. At the NLP Academy we are proud of our training record. The quality of NLP Academy Practitioners and Master Practitioners speaks volumes for our work.

We are proud of all the people who graduate with the NLP Academy and endeavour to support their future development. With the release of the NLPedia Study Sets, we stand alone as the only company in the UK offering genuine multi-sensory home learning packages that support the accelerated learning NLP certification courses.

NLP Application

An NLP Practitioner can employ his/her skills as an agent of change working with individuals, groups, or companies, or even global organizations and governments. As a technology, NLP has an amazing track record for instigating fast and efficient change in individuals and groups.

Many people study NLP to help them become more effective in their chosen field. The patterns can be employed across a wide area of applications ranging from fields as diverse as education, team building, sales, marketing, personal development, leadership and coaching. Wherever there is human interaction and growth potential, NLP can be used to develop and enhance performance.

CHAPTER 16

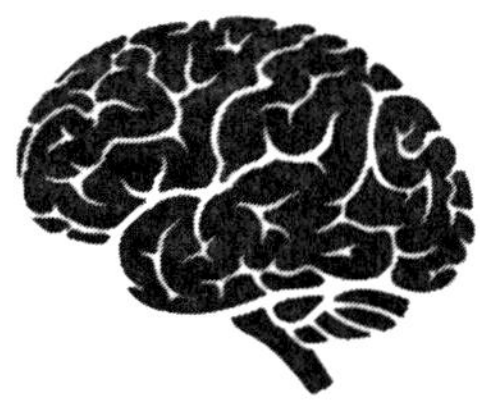

NEURO-LINGUISTIC PROGRAMMING (NLP) CONTD...

What is Neuro-Linguistic Programming?

Neuro-linguistic programming (NLP) is a way of changing our thoughts and behaviors to help achieve desired outcomes. Because our neurological processes, behavior, and language are interconnected, we can "reprogram" our brains to control our thoughts and actions. NLP is also a useful tool for improving communication and developing better relationships.

Who developed Neuro-Linguistic Programming?

Neuro-linguistic programming was developed by information scientist Richard Bandler and linguist John Grinder at the University of California, Santa Cruz in the 1970s. From the very start, NLP was seen as a helpful tool in personal development and has been used extensively ever since. Neuro-linguistic programming has a wide range of applications in counseling, medicine, law, business, sports, and education.

Core Principles of Neuro-Linguistic Programming

Neuro-linguistic programming is based on four core principles:

- Sensory awareness is one of the central elements of neuro-linguistic programming. Being mindful of our own and other people's reactions in any given situation allows us to have more flexibility and control.
- Building rapport refers to creating relationships that are built on mutual trust and understanding. Successful personal and business interactions largely depend on our ability to establish and maintain a rapport with others.
- Outcome thinking helps us direct our thoughts and avoid limiting ourselves by negative thinking. It enables us to make optimal choices and achieve the goals we set for ourselves.
- Behavioral flexibility allows us to change unproductive behaviors, create new perspectives, and build healthy habits.

How does Neuro-Linguistic Programming work?

In Neuro-Linguistic Programming, our minds are perceived as internal operating systems consisting of thoughts, feelings, and beliefs. NLP determines the ways in which our states of mind affect the way we act and communicate with others and, even more importantly, ourselves. These systems can be accessed and changed or "programmed" through language.

Internal maps

Neuro-linguistic programming is based on the idea of internal maps. Internal maps are our personal representations of reality. We learn to navigate these maps through sensory experiences that determine our feelings and behaviors. They can be either auditory, visual, olfactory, gustatory, or kinesthetic. With the help of NLP, it is possible to modify any subconsciously created limitations of our individual maps.

NLP presupposes that we are biased towards one of our sensory systems, whether it is images, feelings, sounds, taste, or smell. Therefore, we tend to use our preferred representational system (PRS) to process our experiences. But if we manage to operate with all the representational systems and make use of the most suitable one in different circumstances, we will succeed in increasing our behavioral flexibility.

Modeling excellence

An important aspect of Neuro-Linguistic Programming is modeling or recreating excellence. Modeling provides strategies for copying the accomplishments of others in order to introduce excellence into our own lives. We can model any skill or behavior by mastering the underlying beliefs and thought processes and applying them to our lives.

Logical levels of change

The model of logical levels of change is an indispensable tool in NLP. It is used to create plans for modifying undesirable thoughts or behaviors.

The model was inspired by renowned British anthropologist and linguist Gregory Bateson. According to Bateson, learning consists of natural hierarchies. These hierarchies provide a roadmap for the change process. Each of the six levels influences and directs the ones below.

Environment

Environment, the setting and people that surround us, is the lowest NLP logical level and the easiest one to modify. Simply changing something in the environment or network can eliminate triggers and modify addictive or obsessive behaviors.

Behaviors

Behaviors often contribute to negative actions and thoughts. It is crucial to be able to identify the unwanted behaviors that should be changed.

Capabilities and skills

Capabilities and skills refer to our ability to make the desired changes, as well as identifying the tools needed to make those changes. Techniques such as meditation, hypnosis, positive thinking, and relaxation can be used in overcoming fears, for instance.

Beliefs and values

Beliefs and values give us internal permission to change. Addictions, obsessions, and other undesirable behaviors can become an important value that negatively affects all the other personal values.

Identity

Identity is an evaluation of our ability to implement changes. It can be either positive or negative.

Purpose and spirituality

Purpose and spirituality pertain to the involvement in religion or ethics, where the change is seen as part of something larger than ourselves.

Does Neuro-Linguistic Programming work for depression?

NLP is commonly used in therapy for treating a wide range of issues from anxiety and phobias to post-traumatic stress disorders and depression. An NLP therapist will try to understand the patient's thinking, behavior patterns, emotional states, and aspirations. By analyzing the individual's internal maps, the therapist can help find and strengthen the most beneficial skills and develop new strategies to replace old, unproductive ones.

Neuro Linguistic Programming Approach and Techniques

NLP therapists use a number of different techniques, including:

Anchoring

Similarly to Pavlov's conditioning, anchoring consists of turning sensory experiences into triggers for a desired emotional state or frame of mind. The anchor can be a gesture like squeezing the thumb and the index finger together or word that is associated with positive emotion. The goal is to be able to immediately access the desired emotional or mental state through the chosen anchor. After some practice, negative emotions can be replaced using these learned triggers.

Swish pattern

Just like anchoring, the swish pattern technique consists of changing response patterns to a situation that causes unwanted behaviors. It can be applied in the cases of anxieties and obsessions, for example. Patients are asked to identify the causes of their problematic behavior. They can then mentally replace the image of the usual response to that trigger by the desired one. With some practice, the new response will be generated automatically whenever the cue occurs and gradually replace the old one.

Visual-Kinesthetic Dissociation

Visual-Kinesthetic Dissociation (VKD), also known as the rewind technique, is useful in eliminating obstructive thoughts and feelings associated with a past event like traumatic memories and phobias. When an event is reimagined and relived from the safe distance of an out-of-body experience, thinking about it will no longer set off unwanted emotions.

Does Neuro-Lingusistic Programming work?

The most significant limitation of NLP is a lack of empirical evidence. Even after several decades of its use, the effectiveness of neuro-linguistic programming and the validity of its theories have not yet been clearly demonstrated by research.

In addition, scientific research on NLP has produced mixed results. Several studies have provided firm proof that it is an effective mode of treatment for mental health issues. At the same time, there is little clinical evidence for the effectiveness of NLP in treating some health-related conditions, such as anxiety disorders, weight management, and addictions.

CHAPTER 17

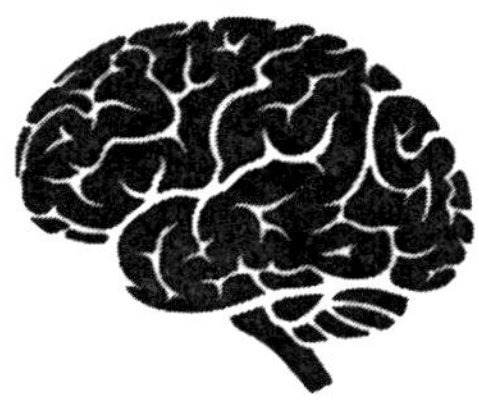

EXPLOITATION OF PSYCHOLOGICAL VULNERABILITIES

Mental health difficulties can affect someone's thought processes, feelings, actions, behaviours and personality.

Everyone experiences times when their mental health is better or worse. Mental health becomes a difficulty if it affects someone's ability to manage day-to-day life.

Mental health problems are hugely varied, as are the effects they have on people. Some people may experience mental health problems for a short amount of time, while for others they may be longer-lasting.

Vulnerability to exploitation

Poor mental health can impact on people's daily life, relationships, social life, employment and finances, making life more challenging and stressful. These impacts may lead to wider issues such as substance misuse, isolation, poor physical health and homelessness. These factors can increase vulnerability to abuse and exploitation.

People experiencing mental health difficulties may seek, or become dependent on, others who can offer them emotional or practical support. The care-giver may use this relationship of trust and dependency to abuse or exploit the individual. They may make their offer of support dependent on the person participating in an exploitative situation, or they may act in a coercive, controlling and violent way.

Mental health difficulties can affect people's ability to tell others that they are being abused or exploited. The nature of their difficulties may make it difficult for them to seek help and support from friends, family and support services. During episodes when their mental health difficulties are particularly severe they may not fully recognize that they are being abused or exploited.

Mental health difficulties may arise from past experience of trauma, abuse or exploitation. The lasting impacts of these experiences on people's lives can increase their vulnerability to further exploitation.

How vulnerabilities can be exploited and what is the purpose of vulnerability scanners?

Vulnerability mitigation is an important topic for any cybersecurity analyst. It is enough to note that the producers with the highest number of detected vulnerabilities are: Microsoft, Oracle, IBM, Google and Apple. Vulnerability is a weakness that an adversary can exploit to breach the confidentiality, availability, or integrity of a resource, and the licensed software we use on a daily basis on our computers is full of them.

Cybersecurity vulnerability refers to implementation flaws or security implications that result from design choices. For example, the possibility of exceeding the buffer limits while writing data to it introduces a buffer overflow vulnerability, the lack of validation of user input exposes the system to SQL-injection attacks, etc. Examples of significant vulnerabilities include Heartbleed, Shellshock/Bash, and POODLE. Several public vulnerability repositories are available that allow interested parties to easily access information on known vulnerabilities.

The most famous vulnerability repositories are:

Common Vulnerabilities and Exploits – CVE's goal is to provide a consistent base of vulnerabilities and common language to cybersecurity analysts. Established in 1999, MITER's public vulnerability repository is approved by the industry through CVE Numbering Authorities (vendors, organizations and researchers actively publishing in the CNA), the CVE council and many products and services based on CVE mitigation. As the creators themselves say – CVE is a dictionary, not a database. The CVE created a vulnerability registration reference system called the CVE identifier (CVE-ID). CVE IDs usually contain a brief description of the security vulnerability, and sometimes advice, mitigation measures, and reports.

National Vulnerability Database – US government repository based on vulnerability management data standards, aggregated using SCAP – Security Content Automation Protocol. This data enables the automation of vulnerability management, security measurement and compliance. The NVD includes references to security checklists, security related software bugs, misconfiguration, product names, and "business" impact indicators. In addition to data collected from SCAP, NVD automatically retrieves data from CVE.

Open Vulnerability and Assessment Language – It is an information security community initiative that aims to standardize how computer systems are assessed and reported on. OVAL includes a language to encode system details and an assortment of content repositories located throughout the community. Tools and services use OVAL for the three stages of system evaluation – representing system information, expressing specific machine states, and reporting evaluation results – provide accurate, consistent, and useful information so that they can improve their security.

Vulnerability management identifies, classifies, assesses and mitigates vulnerabilities. IT security professionals conduct the vulnerability management process in an organized and timely manner by following the steps below:

Preparation: Define the scope of the vulnerability management process.

Vulnerability scanning: Vulnerability scanners are automated tools that scan your system for known vulnerabilities and provide a report of all identified vulnerabilities sorted by severity. Known vulnerability scanners are e.g. Tenable Nessus.

Vulnerability Identification, Classification and Assessment: The Vulnerability Scanner provides a report on the identified vulnerabilities.

Vulnerability Mitigation: The asset owner determines which gaps will be mitigated.

Rescan: After the corrective actions are completed, a rescan is performed to verify its effectiveness. Penetration tests are also often performed at this stage to verify the company's improved IT security posture.

Monitoring and updates

There is some confusion in general public about penetration testing and vulnerability scanning. It's worth emphasizing that the two approaches complement each other, and vulnerability scanning is one of the first steps in a penetration test.

We have already understood what a vulnerability is and how it affects the system – it is a weak spot that can be exploited to gain unauthorized access to a given resource on the network.

So what is an exploit?

An exploit is specially crafted code used by attackers to exploit a certain security vulnerability and compromise the security of resources. This is a vulnerability exploitation tool. The exploit kits are as popular as the exploits themselves. These are tools embedded in attacked websites, which automatically scan the visitor's computer for vulnerabilities and try to use them in real time by selecting an exploit from their database. If the exploit is successful, the kit will introduce malware to the user's system. It is very disturbing for information security professionals that the ease of use and user-friendly interface of the exploit kits allow their deployment also to non-expert users.

Lastly, a vulnerability is a weak spot, and an exploit is a way of using it in the form of a specially prepared source code. There may be dozens, and sometimes even hundreds, of exploits per vulnerability.

CHAPTER 18

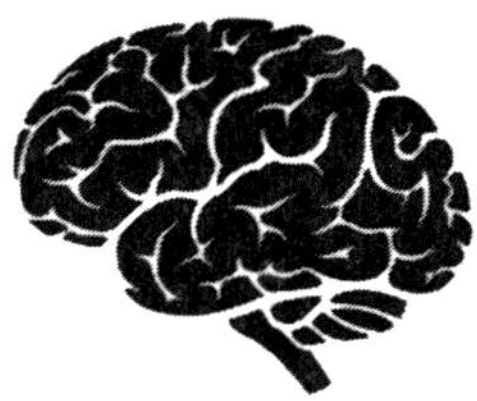

DIFFERENCE BETWEEN PERSUASION AND MANIPULATION

The difference between persuasion and manipulation has been a subject of debate for literally thousands of years. In ancient Greece during the 4th century BC the father of persuasion, Aristotle, opposed a group of teachers known as the Sophists. The Sophists provided instruction in various disciplines, but became infamous for their teaching of rhetoric. Aristotle clashed with the

Sophists over the fact that they did not care about truth, but would promote any idea for a fee. Aristotle asserted that the Sophists were engaging in manipulation because they intentionally deceived people and caused harm.

Today, the debate between persuasion and manipulation rages on. In fact, many confess that they have a hard time distinguishing between the two. Yet, understanding the distinction is vital because it will guide you in influencing others ethically and equip you with the knowledge to recognize manipulative messages.

Why Persuasion is Good?

To accurately discern the difference between persuasion and manipulation it is essential to understand the ethics that undergird persuasion. There are some communication theorists who have declared that persuasion is "ethically neutral." That is to say that persuasion is neither good nor bad, but merely an impartial process. Aristotle stressed that persuasion is inherently good because it is one of the primary means through which truth becomes known. Through the persuasive method an idea is put forth with evidence and a person is allowed to freely choose to either accept or reject that persuasive appeal. Jay Conger wrote about this in the Harvard Business Review, when he affirmed, "Persuasion does indeed involve moving people to a position they don't currently hold, but not by begging or cajoling. Instead, it involves careful preparation, the proper framing of arguments, the presentation of vivid supporting evidence, and the effort to find the correct emotional match with your audience."

The belief that persuasion is an honorable and effective means of arriving at truth is seen by the fact that it is the basis for modern economics, counseling practices and the legal system. In addition, persuasion is also the foundation of democracy. As Professor Raymond Ross writes, "Democracies use thoughtful ethical persuasion whenever they elect leaders, establish laws, or try to protect their citizens." Even those who become dismayed with the notion of persuasion cannot escape it. Persuasion is ingrained within human communication. When communicating, people both intentionally and unintentionally promote certain beliefs and behaviors. Consequently, persuasion is not a matter of choice; it is inherent in social interaction. In fact, it is so pervasive in human communication that at times it becomes almost invisible. Dr. Herbert W. Simons, Professor at Temple University illustrates this when he writes, "The so-called people professions – politics, law, social work, counseling, business management, advertising, sales, public relations, the ministry – might as well be called persuasion professions."

At its core, persuasion is the pursuit of truth. It is through persuasion that positive change occurs. For example, persuasive messages have been scientifically proven to prompt high school students to refrain from smoking, increase lifesaving blood donations, and prevent youth from joining gangs. Communication scholars Gass and Seiter echo this idea when they assert, "Persuasion helps forge peace agreements between nations. Persuasion helps open up closed societies. Persuasion is crucial to the fund-raising efforts of charities and philanthropic organizations. Persuasion convinces motorists to buckle up when driving or to refrain from driving when they've had a few too many drinks. Persuasion is used to convince an alcoholic or drug-dependent family member to seek professional help. Persuasion is how the coach of an underdog team inspires the players to give it their all. Persuasion is a tool used by parents to urge children not to accept rides from strangers or to allow anyone to touch them in a way that feels uncomfortable. In short, persuasion is the cornerstone of a number of positive, pro-social endeavors. Very little of the good that we see in the world could be accomplished without persuasion."

Though, the goodness of persuasion and the fact that it is embedded within human nature is not what causes people concern. What causes anxiety if the corruption of persuasion. To be sure, when persuasion is distorted, it can become manipulative, which is dangerous. Through manipulation, con artists, cult leaders and dictators have abused, enslaved, and even massacred millions. However, as detrimental as manipulation is, it should never be confused with persuasion. Manipulation is the perversion of persuasion. It is not concerned with truth, but rather deceit. Aristotle commented on this in his acclaimed work, Rhetoric when he emphasized, "an abuse of the rhetorical faculty can work great mischief, the same charge can be brought against all good things save virtue itself, and especially against the most useful things such as strength, health, wealth, and military skill. Rightly employed, they work the greatest blessing; and wrongly employed, they work the greatest harm."

Consequently, the pertinent question is how can you distinguish between persuasion and manipulation? There are three reliable ways that you can analyze if a message is manipulative.

Intention

Intention is a primary factor in judging whether a request is manipulative. If a person attempts to present an idea or behavior that is not in the best interest of another, they are engaging in manipulation. Sadly, this is all too common. People frequently fall into the trap of abusing others in the pursuit of what they desire. One of the root causes of this Machiavellian perspective is not viewing others with equality. The renowned philosopher Immanuel Kant wrote about this mindset when he suggested that the foundational precept of morality is treating a person as a human being and not as a thing.

Withholding Truth

Manipulation involves distorting or withholding truth. Often, this is seen through exaggerating the advantages of a behavior, idea or product. It was this form of manipulation that prompted the phrase Caveat Emptor, which is Latin for "Buyer Beware," to become prevalent. The phrase was particularly widespread during those historical periods when there was little accountability for sellers. The saying was a warning to potential buyers to be leery of those selling goods, and to make sure that they verified, before making a purchase, that the quality of the product was identical to the claims made by the seller. Even today most people have experienced being told about the features or benefits of a product or service and then after purchasing it realized that they had been misled. This is wrong, as anything other than honest representation is blatant manipulation.

Coercion

Coercion is the third and most obvious component of a manipulative appeal. It is the removal of free choice, the ultimatum – do it or else. In contrast, persuasion involves influence, but never force. As communication scholar Dr. Richard Perloff writes, "a defining characteristic of persuasion is free choice. At some level the individual must be capable of accepting or rejecting the position that has been urged of him or her." Therefore, an invitation that one is unable to say no to is not persuasive in nature, but is coercive and accordingly manipulative.

Lastly, there is a vast difference between persuasion and manipulation. Persuasion advances the position of all involved. It is a pro-social endeavor that guides the receiver of a message in accepting truth. In contrast, a manipulative appeal is one that if adopted will negatively impact another. Manipulation is morally wrong and ultimately counterproductive to the interests of all involved. As social psychologist Robert Cialdini stated, "The systematic use of misleading influence tactics... ultimately becomes a psychologically and financially self-damaging process." Therefore, through an accurate and robust understanding of both the rightness of persuasion and the three primary elements of manipulation you will be better able to persuade others ethically and protect yourself from manipulative requests.

Body Language in Persuasion

Body language is an important factor in persuasion, as it conveys confidence and trust in the message being passed to the other person. Confidence is the most important aspect in persuasion, as it makes people more likely to believe in the authority of the speaker. To be persuasive, one must master the important contributing factors such as confidence, eye contact, body language, manner of speaking, tone, facial expressions, and general demeanor.

Persuasion is a valuable skill that can be used to improve relationships, get paid what you deserve, and convince others to listen to your advice. Mastering daily affirmations and visualizing the situation can help to prepare for difficult conversations and increase your persuasive abilities.

To persuade people, you need to understand their simple desires, establish a rapport, and help them with self-affirmation. To successfully influence and control the behavior of others, professionals use a variety of methods and techniques, such as hypnosis, combined with knowledge of human psychology and personal characteristics.

CHAPTER 19

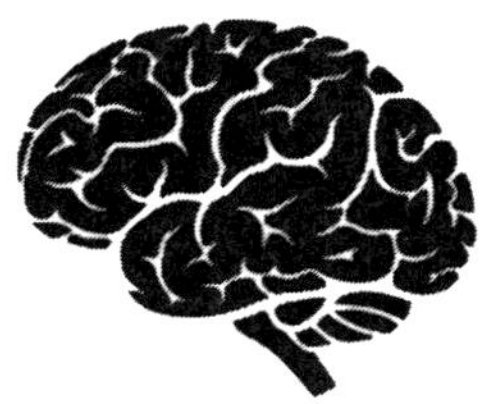

WHAT IS MEDIA MANIPULATION?

Media manipulation is a series of related techniques in which partisans create an image or argument that favors their particular interests. Such tactics may include the use of logical fallacies, manipulation, outright deception (disinformation), rhetorical and propaganda techniques, and often involve the suppression of information or points of view by crowding them out, by inducing other people or groups of people to stop listening to certain arguments, or by simply diverting attention elsewhere.

Mass Media Manipulation Methods

Activism

Activism is the practice or doctrine that has an emphasis on direct vigorous action especially supporting or opposing one side of a controversial matter. It is quite simply starting a movement to affect or change social views. It is frequently started by influential individuals but is done collectively through social movements with large masses. These social movements can be done through public rallies, strikes, street marches and even rants on social media.

Advertising

Advertising is a form of promotion that seeks to persuade a certain audience to purchase a good or service. One of the first types of marketing, it aims to persuade its target market to either buy, sell or carry out a particular action. This tends to be done by businesses who wish to sell their product by paying media outlets to show their products or services on television breaks, banners on websites and mobile applications.

These advertisements are not only done by businesses but can also be done by certain groups. Non-commercial advertisers are those who spend money on advertising in a hope to raise awareness for a cause or promote specific ideas. These include groups such as interest groups, political parties, government organizations and religious movements. Most of these organizations intend to spread a message or sway public opinion instead of trying to sell products or services. Advertising can not only be found on social media, but it is also evident on billboards, newspapers, magazines and even word of mouth.

Hoaxing

A hoax is something intended to deceive or defraud. Misleading public stunts, scientific frauds, false bomb threats and business scams are examples of hoaxes.

Propagandizing

Propagandizing is a form of communication that is aimed at influencing the attitude of a community toward some cause or position by presenting only one side of an argument. Propaganda is commonly created by governments, but some forms of mass communication created by other powerful organizations can be considered propaganda as well. As opposed to impartially providing information, propaganda, in its most basic sense, presents information primarily to influence an audience. Propaganda is usually repeated and dispersed over a wide variety of media in order to create the chosen result in audience attitudes. While the term propaganda has justifiably acquired a strongly negative connotation by association with its most manipulative and jingoistic examples (e.g. Nazi propaganda used to justify the Holocaust), propaganda in its original sense was neutral, and could refer to uses that were generally benign or innocuous, such as public health recommendations, signs encouraging citizens to participate in a census or election, or messages encouraging persons to report crimes to the police, among others.

Propaganda uses societal norms and myths that people hear and believe. Because people respond to, understand and remember more simple ideas this is what is used to influence people's beliefs, attitudes and values.

Psychological Warfare

Psychological warfare is sometimes considered synonymous with propaganda. The principal distinction being that propaganda normally occurs within a nation, whereas psychological warfare normally takes place between nations, often during war or Cold War. Various techniques are used to influence a target's values, beliefs, emotions, motives, reasoning, or behavior. Target audiences can be governments, organizations, groups, and individuals.

This tactic has been used in multiple wars throughout history. During World War II, the western Allies, expected for the Soviet Union would drop leaflets on the US and England. During the conflict with Iraq, American and English forces dropped leaflets, with many of the leaflets telling the people how to surrender. In the Korean war both sides would use loud speakers from the front lines. In 2009, people in Israel in the Gaza war received text messages on their cell phones threatening them with rocket attacks. The Palestinian people were getting phone calls and leaflets warning them that they were going to drop rockets on them. These phone calls and leaflets were not always accurate.

Public Relations

Public Relations (PR) is the management of the flow of information between an individual or an organization and the public. Public relations may include an organization or individual gaining exposure to their audiences using topics of public interest and news items that do not require direct payment. PR is generally created by specialized individuals or firms at the behest of already public individuals or organizations, as a way of managing their public profile.

Media Manipulation Techniques

Using Emotions

It is very simple. When you read a headline that has a strong emotional impact on you then you have already been manipulated. You will read or listen to the rest of the news with the attitude which author of the text wanted you to have. For example, you may become outraged after reading the title, "Police officer brutally overpowered 14-year-old

Asian girl. " Then you will read the rest of the article with your blood pressure raised and anger directed towards the cop. But what if it turns out that the police officer who forcibly knocked a 14-year-old girl to the ground and cuffed her saved the life of her colleague to whom she ran with a knife in her hand with the intention of hurting her?

Asking close questions at the beginning of a news

"Has John Smith stole his grandmother's money?" This question, by how it is formed, already created suspicion connected with the person who's name is used in it. Even though the article does not explain who is guilty of the crime the wording of the headline still makes us negative about John Smith. The point of the author is not to prove his guilt but to create reader's distrust to him.

Surveys

Any of us who has ever seen percentage diagrams, bars or tables can say that these numbers affect one's opinion even more than any six-digit numbers. The percentage of different points of view on one thing is strong manipulation method. Additionally, a short text describing the presented survey results convinces us even more. For example, "in presented survey 90 percent of Poles said that party X is much better than party Y." However, it is hard to agree with this statement when it turns out that the survey was conducted on only 100 representatives of a country which population is around 38 million.

Taking statements out of context

What are your emotions when you hear a statement of president of your country saying "It is impossible to fight with this epidemy. Who is supposed to die, let him die. We can't do anything about that"? What if those words are true, and he really said that? This might not to be a lie. But what if at the beginning of this sentence he said: "In our country there are politicians who think..." and it was just cut off? Does it change your attitude towards him?

Building negative associations

The images speak stronger than words. And this fact is used in media very often. Some news authors combine text with a picture which doesn't show a person described in the article but builds negative image of her. For example, in one of the articles in Polish newspaper an author described a court hearing of one of the nuns and placed a picture of old, malicious, angry lady wearing habit and looking at the reader. In fact, that was not the face of nun which the article was presenting. Even though, for people reading that text and looking at the picture it started to be obvious that she may be terrible, unpleasant person and must be guilty of the crime.

Invoking authority

A gentleman in white medical apron shown on TV said that you should avoid coffee and eat more tomatoes? Ok, so he is a doctor and must know the truth! A quote in newspaper saying "Those who are against immigrants are evil and should not call themselves human" was described as words of world famous writer? Then ... he can't be wrong!

One of the most popular manipulation techniques is invoking authorities, so using a quote of as person who you should listen to, as he or she knows something better than you because of his/her position. It doesn't mean that medical experts are not right when it comes to the health but media use them very often to slide their own point of view inside your mind.

Thus we can see there are many manipulation techniques that are used every day by hundreds of journalists, reporters or influencers. We should know them well to be able to avoid their influence and be aware of the fact that those people want us to think about some things in their specific way.

CHAPTER 20

THE ROLE OF DEFENSE

Acceptance is an important step in building defenses against manipulation, as it allows us to confront reality and make peace with it, instead of denying it and becoming vulnerable to malicious people.

Self-acceptance is a crucial form of acceptance that involves being satisfied with oneself and increasing awareness to identify and defend against manipulation.

Detaching with love is a defense against manipulation that encourages showing love and compassion for others without taking responsibility for their actions, while increasing self-awareness helps to understand one's own personality and values, making it harder for a manipulator to alter thoughts and perceptions.

Detaching with love is an important self-help technique to build self-esteem and defend against manipulation by being kind to oneself, challenging negative thoughts, and avoiding comparison with others.

To defend against manipulation, one must change their reactions by approaching situations with calm rationality, refraining from lashing out angrily, and taking a deep breath to center themselves and create a better response.

Assertiveness is the key to successfully dealing with manipulators, as it involves communicating respectfully while advocating for one's own needs, drawing boundaries, and using effective non-verbal cues.

Eating the right balance of nutrients, such as carbohydrates, omega-3 fatty acids, vitamin B and vitamin D can help improve self-esteem and prevent depression.

Autonomy is having your own identity and being the only one that controls it, and it is highly correlated with happiness. To maintain autonomy and improve self-esteem, be careful about who you choose to date and associate with, and retain control over your life by holding onto foundational values.

Set aside some "me time" for yourself, draw clear personal boundaries, and learn to say "no" to people in order to take control of your life and protect your identity from manipulative people.

CHAPTER 21

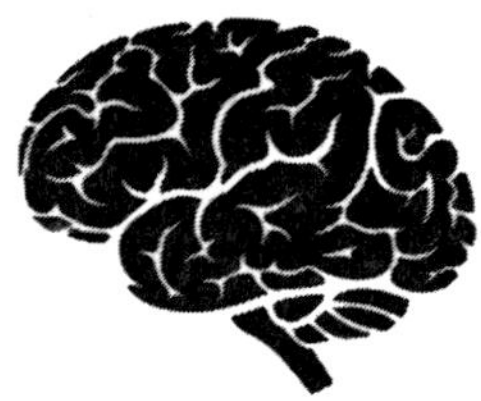

BRAINWASHING

Brainwashing is one way of emotional abuse in relationships. Some narcissistic partners do engage in brainwashing tactics. It is one way of trying to gain control over a person's mind. Narcissistic partners generally try to restrict, control or alter the thoughts of their victims.

Brainwashing is a gradual process of replacing the ideas of a victim with a manipulator about their being and of replacing them with new ideas that can be used to control an individual or a group, often seen in cults where the leader is characterized by their great influence and charismatic behavior.

Ideological brainwashing is a dangerous tactic used by manipulators to control the minds of individuals, typically those in search of fulfillment, by replacing their existing beliefs with those of the manipulator's for their own benefit.

A manipulative person will use clever peripheral associations, demonstrations of utopias, and gradual disclosure to establish trust and manipulate their target, often resulting in the victim feeling a sense of pleasure and acceptance, and being too invested to leave.

Brainwashing has severe psychological effects on victims, such as identity loss, post-traumatic stress disorder, and an inability to escape the manipulator's control.

There are many ways in which brainwashing occurs in human relationships. The first step is love bombing followed by threatening, blackmailing, withholding, withdrawing, dominating, assaulting, criticizing, manipulating, degrading, blaming and even torturing.

Love Bombing

Love bombing is one method of brainwashing. If your partner tries to overwhelm you with loads of affection and gives you too much of attention, you must suspect his or her intentions. Also, showering expensive gifts too frequently could be a love bombing tactic. They do it just to keep you locked up in the relationship without going anywhere else.

Degradation

If your partner tries to degrade you and kill your self-esteem, it could be a tactic of brainwashing. Sarcastic remarks, too much of criticizing, belittling, screaming, humiliating, threatening and verbally attacking to make you feel guilty are all signs of abuse. They do it in an attempt to gain control over you.

Verbal Assaults

If your partner tries to find flaws in you or tries to exaggerate your flaws every moment then it is just an attempt to control your mind and make you feel inferior.

Emotional Blackmail

When your partner threatens you with a break up too frequently, it is one way of psychologically blackmailing you to get something done by you. He or she wants to instill fear in you.

Dominance

At the end of the day, the main purpose behind brainwashing someone is to feel powerful or obtain control over the other. If your partner tries to have the last word in every conversation, it is nothing but brainwashing.

Anxiety

Creating anxiety is one weapon that people who brainwash use. Unreasonable demands, bullying and creating fear are common actions that brainwashing people take.

Unrealistic Standards and Expectations

They expect too much and if you don't live up to the standards, they make you feel like a useless person. That is just a way to brainwash you and make you feel guilty.

Isolation

They isolate you from others so that you will not have enough access to other sources which may make you realize that you are being brainwashed or abused.

Exploitation

There are husbands who brainwash their wives and exploit them financially, emotionally and physically. And there are some wives who brainwash their husbands and make them slog day in and day out to afford a luxurious living. So, exploitation is one motive behind a person who gets into brainwashing.

Symptoms of Brainwashing

Emotional outbursts, arguments, lots of drama, sudden changes in mood, violent behavior and constant anxiety are some symptoms that show up in a person who tries to abuse you in relationship.

How a Brainwasher hides?

After testing your patience and limits, suddenly the person showers you with lots of love and affection. They do it when you reach a breaking point where you want to run out of the relationship. This is just to make you feel good and remain in the relationship. It is unhealthy to stay in such a relationship.

Brainwashing in Abusive Relationships

Being in an abusive relationship often feels like torture. Sometimes that's because your partner's behavior feels like the torture techniques used by mortal enemies instead.

Brainwashing is defined in the Psychology dictionary as that which "manipulates and modifies a person's emotions, attitudes, and beliefs." It reduces a person's ability to mentally defend themselves and makes it easier for another person to control them.

Brainwashing is one example of how abuse in relationships parallels torture. Brainwashing makes it easier to control a targeted person. And it makes it harder for the person to see their way free of the relationship.

Abusive people often are able to throw the targets of their abuse into a trance that makes it difficult for them to think clearly. Targets of abuse can begin to take on the opinions of the abusive person and lose themselves.

A man or woman who is peppered with their partner's opinion, given little or no time to recover, and kept busy responding to demands may not have much mental energy left over. They may be inundated with the partner's version of events to the point where it is difficult to hold on to their own perspective. The anxiety that can be produced by being the target of abuse also makes it difficult to think clearly.

In 1956, Albert Biderman studied how prisoner of war camp personnel got U.S. prisoners of the Korean War to give them tactical information, collaborate with propaganda, and agree with false confessions. Biderman stated that inflicting physical pain was not necessary to "induce compliance," but psychological manipulations were extremely effective for that purpose. His report included what has come to be known as **"Biderman's Chart of Coercion."**

Biderman's chart has been used by many to describe the elements that contribute to brainwashing in various situations, including partner abuse. The tactics included in his chart can be linked to other ways people abuse their partners.

In his Chart of Coercion, Biderman summarized the mechanisms for brainwashing:

- Isolation

- Monopolization of perception (fixes attention on immediate predicament; eliminates "undesirable" stimuli)
- Induced debilitation; exhaustion
- Threats
- Occasional indulgences (provides motivation for compliance; hinders adjustment to deprivation)
- Demonstrating superiority
- Degradation
- Enforcing trivial demands

Not all eight elements need to be present in order for brainwashing to occur. Each element can have some power to distort reality, interfere with perception, reduce a person's self-confidence, and garner compliance.

In a prisoner of war camp, the prisoner and jailer are enemies. Servicemen and women are commonly trained to deal with brainwashing tactics in case they are captured by enemy forces.

CONCLUSION

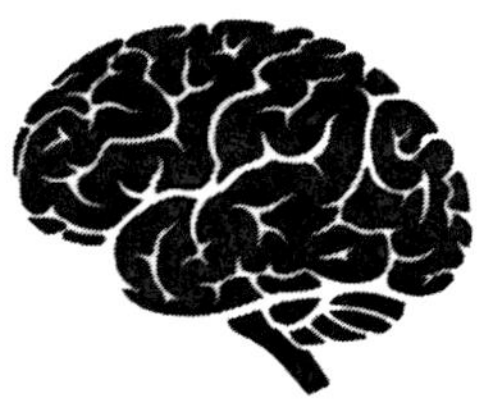

Dark psychology does not allow anyone to surreptitiously control people's minds, at will, and against the targets' will. So, what is dark psychology, instead?

Dark Psychology for Social Manipulation

Dark psychology in social settings consists of strategies and techniques to manipulate people to do what's good for the dark psychologist, but harmful for the victims. We can differentiate between the psychology of persuasion and the psychology of manipulation.

The difference between persuasion and manipulation is that persuasion does not necessarily harm the target of persuasion or, at least, the persuader is not out to willingly harm the target of his persuasion. Manipulation instead entails a loss for the victim of manipulation. That loss can be financial, material, emotional, or loss in his personal power or freedom.

In short, persuasion does not harm people, while manipulation does. At times, that line can be up to interpretation and framing, and persuasion and manipulation can also overlap.

For example, the Nike marketing department might say that they are doing a good thing by making the customers happy with a great product. Someone else might say that Nike is manipulating people to overpay for pieces of poor quality plastics. The same can be said for McDonald's marketing department, or for a pastry shop.

But the line between persuasion and manipulation is not infinitely elastic and, many times, it's pretty easy to differentiate between persuasion and manipulation.

For example, it would much harder for a tobacco company to frame themselves as "helping people enjoy life."

And it's next to impossible for an abusive man to convincingly make the case that his manipulations for relationship control is for "helping his partner staying with the high-quality man he is."

Manipulative Dark Psychology Techniques

Some examples of manipulative techniques that dark psychologists might use:

Manipulative negotiation techniques: How manipulation is used to gain an advantage in negotiations?

Guilt trip power move: When you have no real power, use this "pity play" to make people feel bad and do what you want out of guilt.

Social scalper: Inflate what you did for others to acquire more social-exchange credits than you're due. This one exploits the reciprocity principle to get back more than you've given.

Feminist manipulation: Tell other women to be strong and independent, so that dating gets harder for the target, but easier for the manipulator.

Dark Psychology in Seduction

Dark psychology in seduction seeks bonds and attachments based not on mature love and affection, but on traumatic bonds that leverages or creates psychological wounds

Some examples include:

Regression seduction: Seduction through mother/ father roles

Judge seductions: The individual frames himself as superior, and makes the partner chase for his approval

Traumatic bonding: The individual makes their partner attached through physical and/or emotional abuse

Emotional roller-coaster bonding: The individual makes their partner attached through cycles of fights and re-pacification

Control through personal kinks: The dark psychologist can provide sexual satisfaction through kinks that the target keeps secret. The dark psychologist becomes the only person that can sexually satisfy them, plus they acquire an important secret the target wishes to keep secret, which gives them leverage

Love bombing: The individual seeks to make the partner feel special and unique through a showering of endless attention and adulation.

Some of the above techniques are sometimes deployed subconsciously, and sometimes they are even the natural consequence of an individual's psychological makeup, as it's the case with the anxious-avoidant attachment, for example.

But some other times, they are premeditated. Love bombing, for example, tends to be more premeditated.

Dark Psychology in Relationships

Dark psychology in relationships applies psychological principles to gain power and control one's partner.

For example, each partner can gain by keeping one nominally committed relationship, with all the sexual and emotional benefits that entails, while also seeking more sex on the side -and that's why cheating exists.

Dark Psychology in Politics

Dark psychology in politics consists of techniques of propaganda and political debating designed to negatively frame one's opponent, influence voters, and enduce citizens to abandon individualistic behavior in favor of the collective.

There are many levels of political dark psychology, and we can separate them into two major groups: during campaigns, and in office.

In democracies, these two phases can overlap since politicians in power are still campaigning for the next elections.

But even in democracies, you can still notice a marked switch from campaign to office.

During campaigns

- Frame the opponent as ineffective and unworthy
- Frame the current state as hopeless
- Frame yourself as the man to fix the situation
- In extreme situations, make up an enemy and paint yourself as the right person to destroy that enemy

Once in power

- Frame the status quo as positive
- Take personal credit for things going well
- Find scapegoats for things going poorly
- Foster ideals of nationalism to drop rational selfishness in favor of the group (which ultimately benefits the politicians who lead those groups)

The last stage is common in many groups.

Government officials indeed can be seen as group leaders. And in the case of extremist governments, despots act the same way as cult leaders and hate groups leaders act, using the same principles of dark psychology.

That includes:

- Making up enemies
- Increasing group cohesion through extremist values and religious zealot
- Stoking fears and framing oneself as the only one to effectively tackle the danger

- Stoking anger as a diversion tactic

Dark Psychology in Groups

Dark psychology seeks to reduce the followers' power and independence, while increasing the leaders' power and control.

Because most group leaders want to decrease members' power and independence while increasing their power and influence over those same group members.

To make people more dependent on the group, group leaders will deploy several tactics of dark psychology, including:

Make people's problems appear as bigger than they actually are: So people believe they will need the group and group leader to solve them

Ridicule, disempower, or exclude discording voices: Cult leaders seek to cut out all discordant opinions. Since that's rarely possible, group leaders frame any discordant voices as "idiotic", "uninformed", or "manipulative" so that they can inoculate their effect and keep followers loyal to the group's diktats and dogmas.

More dark psychology techniques in groups are:

- **Fostering group's superiority over the individual:** Humanist and enlightened ideals of individualism and personal freedom are a threat to group leaders. They seek instead to prioritize the group over any individual. The more people sacrifice themselves for the group, the more power they have.
- **Dissolving members' ego with the group:** The more members identify with the group, the more power the group -and the group leader- will have on its members

- **Fusing the group with the leader:** The last stage of dark psychology is for the leader to embody the group. That way, he can reach total control over its members. At that point, there is no group anymore, just the leader and its followers who are in it for the leader.

Dark Psychology in War

Dark psychology seeks to instill terror, to mentally dominate or unsettle the enemy in a way that will handicap its fighting ability and, ideally, to make their fight and resistance seem futile.

Manipulative communication during war frames the enemy as barbaric, and brutal, and spreads that view as widely as possible.

Dark Psychology on the Air

During wartime, psychology is even more effectively deployed to control and sway public opinion. Wartime manipulation consists of five different elements:

- **Frame oneself as "good":** Ideally, as "holy", or as having a responsibility to export "good" wherever you're going to fight
- **Frame the enemy as evil**: The enemy is oppressive, brutal or, even better, a threat to our way of life or our own same existence
- **Make victory seem easy and obvious**: Few people want to actually go fight that war. So make it seem like a quick and easy business
- **Hide the true costs of war**: Nobody wants to pay for that war. So hide the costs, make it seem like the people will gain from it

- **Hide the true emotional costs:** Nobody wants to see that our holy war is bringing death and suffering. So hide the casualties, the mothers with dead children, and the children crying on the bodies of their dead parents.

Motivating Operations (Mo') Power, (Mo') Manipulation

Dark Psychology can provide the cover for brutality to keep going unchecked. Countries with bigger budgets engage in dark psychology to control what the world thinks of their wars.

By dominating the informational war, more powerful countries can keep engaging in modern-day colonialism and invasions without people realizing what they're truly up to.

For example, few people in the West would think of Israel as a bullying, invading force. That's because many major media outlets frame Israel as a victim, and Palestinian fighters are often referred to as "terrorists".

Dark Psychology in Business

Dark psychology in business manipulates employees into giving up their individual self-interest in favor of the organization, while accepting only a small portion of their true contribution.

Dark psychology is not a formal and recognized branch of psychology. There is no such thing as research labeled as "dark psychology", or any formal education courses on it.

That's why if you research it on the web you get a lot of dubious sites and books on the topic. However, that is not to say that dark psychology itself is ineffective, or wholly unsubstantiated.

Dark psychology is effective because dark psychology is psychology. Dark psychology is simply psychology - and social sciences in general - applied for harmful and abusive ends.

People have been manipulating each other since antiquity by playing on simple innate human emotions to get what they want. By learning the tricks of the trade when it comes to picking up non-verbal communication and body language, one can gain an advantage over others in any situation.

*****